TWILIGHT OVER THE WILDERNESS

TWILIGHT OVER THE WILDERNESS

By OLAV WALLO

With 27 Full Color Paintings

By ROGER PREUSS

Member Society of Animal Artists
Fellow International Institute of Arts

Publishers

T. S. DENISON & COMPANY, INC.

Minneapolis, Minnesota

 T. S. DENISON & COMPANY, INC.

All rights reserved, including the right to reproduce this book, or portions thereof, except that permission is hereby granted to reviewers to quote brief passages in a review to be printed in magazines and newspapers, or for radio and television reviews.

Standard Book Number: 513-01210-9
Library of Congress Card Number: 70-16085-4
Printed in the United States of America
by The Brings Press
Copyright © MCMLXXI by T. S. Denison & Co., Inc.
Minneapolis, Minn. 55437

Acknowledgments

We acknowledge with appreciation the paintings included by permission in this volume from collections, except as otherwise noted, of *The Thos. D. Murphy Company,* Red Oak, Iowa, and the *Wildlife of America® Gallery*, Minneapolis, Minnesota.

Dedication

This book is dedicated to the trail blazers in conservation, to the pioneers for the preservation of our wildlife and the priceless resources of America; to the friends of our wilderness who like simple things, the true things, Nature's way of doing things. These men and women have been guardians of our rich and beautiful land. The roads they have wandered for many years have been long and cumbersome. Often there was failure, sacrifice and tears. Their struggle has been against overwhelming odds, but they never gave up. My humble thanks to those stouthearted people that had the foresight and courage to defend and preserve our American Heritage.

—Olav Wallo

Introduction

From the beginning hunting and fishing was a way of life to the American Indians. But they did not despoil their bounty nor did they ravage the habitat necessary to sustain wildlife. They cherished it, guarded it and took only what was needed to sustain themselves.

Now there are too many of us and we are laying waste to the soil, the waters, the forests and wildlife that was our wealth when the Pilgrims first set foot on America's shores. Pitiably few people now even think about this heritage and about our environment, but the number who cares is growing, albeit at a painfully slow pace.

One of these is an ex-patriot from Norway—Olav Wallo—who in this book seeks to warn us of our extravagant, wasteful and insensible ways. Yet he brings us a message of hope, too, straight from his beloved Norway and in Sweden where wildlife is so prized and preserved that moose still survive in harvestable numbers (some 45,000 a year as the hunter's share).

But in America today how many of us have heard the haunting voice of the wolf, or the wild laughter of a loon, or even the soul-stirring honking of Canada geese? All are the sounds of a fast-disappearing wilderness, bowing before the onslaught of a careless civilization.

How soon will they all be stilled forever? Olav Wallo doesn't know, but he fears it may be sooner than you think unless we get the message; and in this book he tries—we think expertly—to awaken your sense of kinship with the earth and its wild things.

He is a conservationist first, last and always, and he is a humanitarian. He abhors needless suffering, among wildlife as among humans. So there are chapters here that could offend some segments of society—the trappers, the bow and arrow enthusiasts and yes, even the trophy hunters. But Olav Wallo believes that time yet remains, if we act now, to save the priceless heritage of wildlife that was ours when the first settlers arrived.

It has been done in Norway and Sweden, and the author senses it can be done here—if we properly educate our youth to the values and the delicacies of the interrelationship of wildlife species, including man. And if we stop plundering the land on which these species live.

It is a ringing cry in the wilderness, pleading for man to understand and appreciate his wildlife heritage. Any hunter, any fisherman, any conservationist, and especially the youths, will be interested.

—JACK CONNOR
Former outdoor writer for
The Minneapolis Star and Tribune

Contents

	PAGE
Our American Heritage	17
The Experts	21
Nature's Wonderland	32
The Brown Bear Hunter	53
Can the Nine Mile Creek Be Saved?	59
The Nuisance Hunter and Trapper	64
Conservation	65
The Virgin Wilderness	67
The Sports Hunter	70
The Bow-and-Arrow Hunter	76
Trapping Wild Animals	85
The Trophy Hunter	88
The Meat Hunter	91
The Polar Bear Hunter	92
Joe the Deer Hunter	99
The Happy Wanderer	102
Todde the Raccoon	106
A Letter to the President of the United States	109
The Timber Wolf	119
A Gruesome Sight	124
Wolves' Heaven	125
On Wildlife Management	128
Justice for All	130
Deer Snaring in the North Woods	134
Farewell to the Prairie Chicken	135
A Journey on the Lonesome Trail	140
In Appreciation	141

Paintings by ROGER PREUSS

	PAGE
Canada Geese—Feeding Time	21
The Brook Trout	32
Bear Creek Fisherman	53
"Along the Creek"	59
Ruffed Grouse at Sundown	70
Pheasants in an Autumn Marsh	80
The Intruder—Cottontails	85
The Elk	88
The Mule Deer	99
The Smallmouth Bass	102
Night Watch—Raccoons	106
"Canvasbacks at Lake Christina"	109
The Prairie Chicken	135
Monarch of the Wilderness	Cover Painting
The First Flush—Bobwhite	Back Cover Painting

GALLERY OF PAINTINGS 142

The Homemakers—Mourning Doves
The White-Tailed Ptarmigan
The White-Tailed Deer
Largemouth Bass—Feeding Time
The Mountain Goat
The Badger

The Moose
The Bobcat
The Mountain Quail
The Prairie Dog
The Striped Skunk
The Red Fox

Foreword

From the darkest ages, from the first gleam of man as a human being, from the first page in civilization's history, man and wildlife have wandered over the earth—not as friends but as enemies. For man to live off the land it was necessary to kill and eat wild animals and birds. Their lives were sacrificed so that the human race could live and progress.

The killing of wild animals through the ages has been brutal and gruesome with very little emphasis on a quick and painless death. Even today, as civilized nations, our methods have not improved much. The relation between the hunters in the United States and our wildlife suggests a big arena, in the center of which the animals stampede in a circle, trying to escape from their worst enemy, the human race. All around the ring are hunters and other people, big and small, all trying to deliver a telling blow—using anything from a knife to a sharp arrow, from a small caliber gun to a powerful rifle. There is no restriction, no law on hunting gear. Anything that can draw blood and hurt animals is approved. It all depends upon chance and the hunter's choice of weapons. Some hunters do not consider the wildlife a creation of God or a fellow creature, but as an enemy that must be destroyed as soon as possible. We shudder when at a bullfight we see the matador jab his sword into the bull's body. We claim it is inhuman, that it is barbarous. But we think nothing of sending an arrow into a wild animal or bird, and in this instance, maybe after days, even months, the poor creature finally gasps its last breath in agony and pain.

Then there are those steel animal traps, gruesome inventions, a shameful disgrace to civilized nations. Something is terribly wrong. On one hand we are the most generous people on earth. We contribute billions of dollars to underprivileged countries, to the poor and the hungry. If a catastrophe strikes any place in the world, we are there with a whole army of ships and airplanes carrying food and clothing to restore the everyday life of the stricken people. Why is it that we have no heart and soul and are so brutal in our dealings with our wildlife?

The answer is quite simple. Throughout our lives we have never learned to respect, honor and sympathize with wild animals. For many persons, the inhabitants of the wilderness are of no importance and they could just as well be destroyed. When a child folds his tiny hands in the evening and asks God to bless his father, mother and home (maybe Rover also) there is never a thought about the wilderness, the hunted and mistreated wildlife. The thought is that everyone has the right to destroy wildlife.

The time has come to turn over a new leaf in this nation's progress and learn an important lesson in the conservation of our wonderful wildlife. Concern for wild game should be taught in the homes and schools. The time to start is *now* before many more of our wild species disappear, never to return.

We must not harbor the faulty conclusion that the wildlife and the wilderness will remain as at present, in quantity and area. If the population explosion cannot be controlled, then sometime in the future cities will have standing room only. We are now entering the twilight period when we can still enjoy our fellow creatures and a beloved, unspoiled region. But it will last only a few years. It is as though the faithful friends of wildlife and the wilderness gathered on the shore of a peaceful fjord for the last time, to see the gorgeous sunset, to hear the final chimes from the evening bells floating over the still water, and to see the last golden sunbeams mirrored in the crystal-clear fjord—like pillars of shining coins. Soon the sun sinks below the horizon and the long shadows creep over the landscape, covering it with a gray veil. Then the wilderness vanishes and the wildlife fade into the black, eternal night.

* * *

From the enormous glaciers in the north, over tundras wide and endless, came the ice floes, pressing south. There were billions of tons of ice grinding over the surface of the earth with thunderous roars, pressing out between high mountains, ripping out big chunks of solid rock, flattening hills, filling ravines and leveling the contour in front.

But in the wake of the ice were many small and large valleys and holes. Sliding over the wide prairie and flat land, the ice finally came to a grinding halt in the south. The sun melted the ice in the valleys, ravines and the holes on the prairies. Foglike steam covered the ice floes. Small creeks dribbled out of the full lakes, soon became streams, then rivers and finally wound their way to the open sea.

Birds with seeds in their beaks and bodies emigrated to the new land. Grass sprang up, trees grew, flora covered the landscape. Fauna streamed in and a rich life began in a newborn region.

Next came the red man, a hardy and strong tribe roaming the great country. They hunted and fished and lived off the land; an enormous realm it was. It stretched from the blue Pacific to the Atlantic Ocean.

Later came some freeborn men from a seafaring country, with the glittering shields on their long, smooth Viking ship, breaking the steel-blue waves over the endless ocean. With full sail they searched the shoreline and found a rich, fertile and beautiful country which they called Vinland.

Humble and poor, but with courage and determination, the United States of America came into existence two centuries ago, and since then has made tremendous progress in many fields and projects. It is a saga unparalleled in the history of the world. Within a short time this great country in North America has become the most powerful nation on earth, rich and mighty, but still good-hearted and generous. It is no wonder that this country is the showcase of the world. It is honored and admired by most, ignored by some, disliked by a few. The neighbors and people in faraway lands focus their magnifying glasses and binoculars on this great country. Millions of human beings watch our life and progress in a multitude of fields. Our admitted goal is better living for all and an ascension to higher culture, coupled with a better understanding of the world's problems and wants.

But from many lands and millions of people comes the inquiry: What are the Americans doing for their wildlife? What are they doing with their millions of prairie acres, thousands of lakes and rivers, with their endless wilderness? Are the Americans also the leaders, the trail blazers, in these projects?

This book is written from the point of view of a stranger, standing outside, peering in through a powerful telescope. My knowledge and experience recorded here have been gathered from many lands and throughout many years. I write as a critic, with severity, and let the chips fall where they may. Should I defame anybody unjustly, I hope he will accept my humblest apology. I speak as one of the wilderness' most faithful friends. I have heard the sorrowful call from empty, lonesome trails. I have felt the depressing loss, the dwindling of our wild creatures in the woods. In the still nights I listen to the soft sobs from field and forest, crying for their children. I stand outside looking in, hopefully waiting and watching.

—The Author

Our American Heritage

High and mighty, with lifted torch stands the Statue of Liberty in New York Harbor, a symbol of the United States, its freedom and generous hospitality. Characteristic is the inscription on the statue, as she stands there like a hostess to welcome all to this great country.

"Give me your tired, your poor, your huddled masses, yearning to breath free . . . I lift my lamp beside the golden door."
—Emma Lazarus.

They came by the millions, the strong and the healthy, the sick and the poor, the blond, blue-eyed, and dark-complexioned. Wave after wave they rolled westward. They cleared the woods and grubbed the fields. The prairies' rich soil turned black behind the plow. Iron and coal were dug from the mighty mines. Timber and wood products were cut from the forest. Then there was the endless virgin wilderness with fish-rich rivers, sky-blue lakes and countless wildlife. Our country's wildlife was like a gushing spring for the pioneers, a well of clear, cold water, enough for everybody.

But men became greedy and wasteful. The old oaken bucket was too slow. Then came the stroke pump which was soon exchanged for the new, faster jet pump that never stopped until the well went dry. So today we have millions of acres of field and forest, overwhelmingly big and beautiful, but so empty and lonesome. The citizens of this great country are free and independent, free to hunt-to-kill, wound or even cripple the wild animals. In the past, hunters slaughtered sixty million buffaloes, not for meat or hides alone but just to kill. Next came the buffalo skinners who shot the buffalo for the hides alone and left the carcass to rot on the prairie. Today the buffalo is practically extinct.

It was the same tragic destruction that wiped out the untold millions of passenger pigeons. When the killers were through there were no birds left for tomorrow, the next day or the coming generation. The moose and elk were a common sight in the central and northern portions of the United States in pioneer days. Now there are a few thousand elk cramped in a small territory and a small number of moose in the Northwest. The caribou, so common in many states in the early days, have disappeared, but big herds still roam Canada's and Alaska's endless wilderness. Almost all the bear have been killed off. The prairie chickens' booming call, not so long ago rolled over the wide states in springtime's early morning. That is now almost a thing of the past. Some years ago there were plenty of pheasants in the fields and alongside the roads. It seemed that they were running and flying in all directions. Few are seen now and the pheasant hunters return home empty-handed.

Not long ago the horse-driven binder harvested the wheat, oats and barley on the prairies. The bundles were stacked in shocks for drying. When the grain was dry enough, it was loaded on wagons and hauled to the threshing machine. By this method, lots of kernels were shaken off and left on the ground, which furnished food for the birds in fall and winter. Then a new invention came, the combine, which saved lots of grain. The machine left only a few kernels of grain in a square foot of ground, and even with this the birds did not starve. But the combine was improved every year and soon very little food was left in the fields. The same story is true of the cornhusker, and now more modern machines leave less food for the birds. In yesteryears there were lots of weeds in the fields and along gravel roads and fences to furnish cover and food for the birds. That is a thing of the past. On the farms, in the villages and towns — any place where weeds grow — herbicides are used. These poisons kill not only the weeds but also the wildlife. Nothing can live and reproduce in a poisonous environment. When the shelter of tall, thick weeds is destroyed, pheasants disappear.

We in America are known all over the world for our record-breaking accomplishment in so many fields. We just have got to be the best. Records are to be broken. It must be done. The same holds true in the sad saga of our wildlife. We are only 250 years old as a nation, but in that very short time we have accomplished the impossible. We have slaughtered and destroyed millions of our precious wildlife with very little thought for tomorrow or the next generation. It seems that the universal declaration, the constant sermon, was always for killing. Today we are scraping up crumbs that are left from this brutal, insane time.

If we now in this country will take a long and hard look at the wildlife saga and where we now stand in regard to our future fauna, it will become apparent that the day is not far off when our beautiful wilderness will be a dead and lonesome landscape; and the fields and prairie will be places where game birds no longer exist.

Maybe this is the wilderness' swan song, the last sorrowful taps for the ill-treated wild animals and game birds. It seems unbelievable that it can happen in one of the richest countries of the world, where the living standard is so high. We have excellent schools, colleges and universities. We have symphony orchestras, theaters and operas. We have high culture and so many things to be proud of. But when it comes to hunting, we are savages from way back. If we could go with the game wardens into the field and forests after the fall hunting and see the crippled, badly-wounded animals, those that are blinded and doomed to days of slow starvation, then our belief in the present civilization would be thoroughly shaken. We have very few regulations with regard to hunting gear, caliber of rifles or ammunition. Anybody, from the very young to the very old, anybody who can lift a rifle and pull a trigger, is welcome to buy a hunting license; and the wilderness inhabitants are at his mercy. We have hundreds of deer, dead and decaying in our woods, not from bullet wounds but from shotgun blasts from pheasant hunters' guns. These were not killed for the meat, and the carcass is lying there rotting because the deer season is not yet open.

Here are a few examples from recent game warden reports: "Found eleven deer shot to death by pheasant hunters. Found one big buck standing totally blind from a shotgun blast. Found three deer in a dry creek bed shot to death by arrows. A farmer found a big buck deer standing in his yard that was only skin and bones because he had an arrow lodged in his throat and could not eat or drink. A young doe was found starved to death in a swamp with its hind leg shot off." These examples indicate how bad the situation is today. The number of deer killed or crippled by bullets from small caliber rifles is unknown, but often people wandering through the woods stumble onto a dead deer, a victim of a small bullet, a slow death by bleeding.

There is an old saying: "It is not so much where we now stand, but the important thing is to know where we are going." To the defenders of our wilderness and fauna it seems as though we are not going any place. In fact, we feel that we are retreating step by step—against overwhelming odds. If you are dedicated to the defense of our American heritage, you are playing an important part. The road ahead is long and cumbersome with very little sympathy and understanding from the great majority of our citizens. Our cry against injustice is seldom heard. Sometimes it is like a scream, a voice in the sandy desert where the air is dead and the voice does not carry and the sound will never penetrate. Noah's Ark is still sailing with its precious cargo, but year by year so many of the inhabitants disappear and die, never to return. The ark sails on with less and less cargo. Animals that die and disappear are of little concern to the human race, so it seems. Some day the ruler of all animals, the Human King himself, will step ashore from the ark and find himself alone in a dead and depressing, lonesome world. He will regret with sorrow his stupidity through all those thousands of years. Although he has tremendous knowledge and experience and know-how, he cannot, with all his magic, restore a single species of that departed fauna.

CANADA GEESE—FEEDING TIME

Collection of Wildlife of America

The Experts

He was a tall and strongly built man and walked with long and healthy steps. An outdoor man, he was a forest supervisor in a country that had made great progress in conservation recently. He had woodland's fresh aroma with him wherever he went and the morning sun reflected in his ruddy face. Through many years he had gathered knowledge and experience in the forests, fields and mountains. This wisdom he had collected year after year like autumn leaves stacked upon each other. Now he was recognized as the foremost conservation expert, not only in his homeland of Germany, but in several European countries. He had not accumulated his learning through college and university training, but from nature itself. He had learned, listened to and never forgotten the facts of nature. It had been a long, tiresome struggle with many hardships, setbacks and failures. But now with his two feet planted firmly on the earth, he knew not only the questions but also the answers. When he talked, people listened.

Max Shulls was seventy years young, hardy and healthy. He was touring the United States, although it was not his first trip to America. He had traveled extensively in this country as a young boy. From those days he had always dreamed of returning to this country, as he remembered this fabulous realm with its millions of acres of wilderness, parks, fields, mountains and forests and its wild game in uncounted millions, even more numerous than the stars showering the heavens on a clear autumn night. His biggest interest was conservation, of course, and he was anxious to learn how the United States Conservation Department was operating in comparison with the foremost countries in Europe. His destination was Minnesota where his daughter Heidi lived in Minneapolis.

He was in no hurry. From New York he traveled by bus and stopped for a few days if he discovered an interesting town or place where wild game might be. He inquired about where wild game could be found or asked about hunting and fishing. He was on the move, full of life and energy.

As he hiked the roads and often the forgotten trails, he was always listening and looking for animal tracks in the sand and dirt. He visited the marshes, streams and lakes, counting the wild birds and animals. Often he would seek out the game warden to ask questions about wildlife. He found these men very dedicated to their jobs, but he got the impression that a sadness had settled over them, and they reported they were fighting a losing battle. He had a movie camera ready for use if he found an interesting motif.

From the bus he would glance over the fleeting landscape, endless it seemed, thousands of miles wide by thousands of miles long with numerous forests, lakes, large and small rivers and tall mountains. He also noted that most of the farms were large with big equipment to till the soil and the cattle were plentiful, well fed and healthy. The bus often stopped in small towns with one main street, a few stores and some high grain elevators standing like cathedrals on the prairie. He also visited some cities, but he had a feeling, that made of concrete and steel and glass, they were too large for their own good. A mighty land it was, enormously big and wealthy.

He found the state of Wisconsin interesting. It was beautiful, dressed in the generous color display of autumn. And he also found more and more wildlife here than he had seen so far. Of course, it was nothing to brag about but it was encouraging and he hoped to find more wild game farther north. He had spent two weeks traveling in search of wild game and by now he had a sneaking suspicion that the situation had changed since his first trip to the United States. He had seen very little wildlife.

Minneapolis was bathed in bright October sunshine as the bus rolled into the station. He knew much about this beautiful city because his daughter, Heidi, had sent many pictures and magazines from the Twin Cities with its marvelous parks, streams and lakes. Max also remembered the fine homes surrounded by well-kept lawns with numerous flowers and shrubs.

The reunion of father and daughter was a joyous one. Heidi kept Max busy with dinners and parties in the evenings and sightseeing tours during the day. He loved song and music. He believed they were tonic for a man's soul and he was quite a musician in his own right. One evening he attended one of the season's first symphonies at Northrop Auditorium. His appearance was gentlemanly in his well-tailored tuxedo. The man seated next to Max introduced himself and before the performance, the two were engaged in a lively conversation. The man, Irvin Orby, turned out to be a dedicated conservationist. After the excellent performance with its wonderful singing and music, Max and Irvin had a cup of coffee and discovered they had the same philosophy about conservation. Max was invited to his new friend's home on an island in the northern part of the state.

A few days later Max was on his way to visit Irvin. The bus sped north over fine highways through a beautiful landscape with its changing perspective of blue shimmering lakes and rivers wandering through field and forest, bursting forth with the gushing and bubbling sound of their rapids. At the start the forest was mostly hardwood standing thick and tall, but farther north the evergreens took over with Norway pine and lustrous fir, sprinkled with aspen, mountain ash and bright, friendly birches. Max had a great time and was in excellent humor during the trip; he could never tire of the picturesque moods of the changing landscapes. He had visited many lands but Minnesota had a wealth of so many things that he felt the citizens of this great state must be very proud of their heritage. It was a paradise for the folks and a heaven for wildlife.

At the bus station Irvin greeted Max with a warm welcome and a firm handshake. From the station to the lake was only a short distance, and a tall athletic-looking Indian was waiting for them at the landing. He was dressed in full Indian costume with headgear full of feathers standing erect in their rainbow colors. His name was White Horse but people called him Big Bill. For

Max it was a wonderful experience to meet a full-blooded Indian, a freeborn son of the wilderness. It was also his first time to travel in a canoe. He sat in the middle with Big Bill in the front and Irvin paddling in the back. The day was warm and Big Bill shed his coat and shirt, showing his great physique with muscles like steel-coil springs moving under the red skin. Max noticed that Bill's paddle was twice as wide as Irvin's and when Bill rammed the paddle in the water and pulled with all his might the canoe shot forward sending a fine spray over the bow as it broke the waves.

They were heading for an island not far away which grew in dimension as they approached its thick woods covering the shore. This was Irvin's home, a haven in the wilderness, a precious island in an enormous lake! A pier of logs jutted from the shore. From this landing to the house was a wide path with birch trees standing on either side like an honor guard for the distinguished guest. The house was built of sturdy timber and looked as though it had grown out of the sandy soil. Facing the lake was an enormous fireplace of split cobblestones reflecting brilliant hues. A high tower with large windows on all sides rose from the rooftop. While Bill handled the suitcases, Irvin introduced Max to Victoria, the housekeeper, a woman with brown eyes, black hair and a friendly smile. Most of the furniture was leather-upholstered and rested on a hardwood floor shining white and anchored to the floor beams by wooden pegs.

Dinner was served outside with a breathtaking view of the lake and the surrounding forest, the hills and knolls displayed the manifold autumn colors. It was a memorable occasion for Max and all he could say was "Vunderbar! Vunderbar!" After the meal they moved to some big easy chairs in the house and soon dozed off, tired from the day's toil. A light breeze from the blue lake skimmed through the branches and leaves, collecting and carrying along the woodland's fresh aroma through the open window where the white curtains fluttered, then tiptoeing through the room whispering a lonely tune from the silent wilderness of bygone years.

In the evening the two went on a hike around the large island with its abundance of wildlife. There were not only small animals like squirrels, chipmunks, rabbits, and foxes, but also deer. There were plenty of birds, from little chickadees and creepers to pheasants, ducks and geese. In a clearing in the center of the island they stopped abruptly as overhead came the tremendous noise of wings beating the air. Flock after flock of ducks and geese passed over, numbering in the hundreds. For Max it was the most thrilling sight he had seen in a long time. He was smiling and laughing just like a little boy looking at a wonderful toy, and memories of his first trip to America came suddenly to his mind. He remembered the old-timer who talked about the middle 1800s when ducks by the millions winged their way north to the nesting grounds. Flock upon flock for days and nights, often so numerous they shaded the sun. Geese also by the uncounted thousands headed north in the snowplow formations often a mile wide. At times nothing could be heard so overwhelming was the sound of their honking and wingbeats.

The men walked a little farther and came to a good-sized lake with a number of ducks still swimming on it. On the far side Max spotted Big Bill; he had scared the birds so that Max could enjoy the unusual sight of all those hundreds in flight and the noise of wings beating the air.

After the long hike inspecting Orvik's Island the men were sitting outside the house in the warm evening watching the gorgeous sunset. Flaming red, the sun was like a glowing ball of fire there, sinking below the horizon. It seemed to linger for a short time as though it enjoyed a cold dip in the clear blue lake and then it sank below and disappeared. In the enormous heavens some purple-painted clouds drifted slowly through the west. From the marsh and the weeds and rushes of the bay came the evening haze, rising slowly up and filtering into the last flickering sunbeams. It soon covered the sandy shoreline and the contour of the land was blurred out; only the trees and high knoll were thrust out, looking like a floating island in a gray-colored sea.

All was quiet and only a songbird's trill from a treetop could be heard, a flute-like serenade, a singer's praise to a perfect day of the fleeting summer. A peaceful twilight has settled over nature and soon the wilderness is tucked in—in a silent night of dreams.

After some time the men moved inside and Max was invited to the study in the lookout tower on top of the house. It was not a very big room but it had windows on all sides, and of course a wonderful view over the lake and surrounding territory. The study was full of books and magazines, maps and papers and a driftwood tree root was standing in a corner, and Max knew for certain that he had found a man with an enormous knowledge of conservation, a friend of the wilderness, of wildlife, and a stout defender of the American heritage.

It turned out to be a long evening for Max and Irvin in the lookout tower. In fact, it lasted into early morning. Max had anticipated that many things were wrong with conservation of the natural resources in the United States, but now he got the full impact, facts and figures about what has happened and will happen if the citizens of this great country do not wake up soon.

Max had been wondering what had become of all those ducks and geese that used to wing their way north, and Irvin explained that it is quite simple. "We destroyed thousands of marshes, swamps and potholes, and drained off 3,100 small lakes so that their breeding places are gone and cannot be restored. If you look at this map, you will see the constructed channels fanning out from the rivers, then from the canals the ditches, spreading out like herringbone on both sides of the water courses. All told, we have thousands of miles of dikes crawling into the farm country.

"But you cannot blame the farmer when somebody would inquire if he wanted to raise crops or ducks in his marshes. It certainly was an act of stupidity to drain off the wetland and wrest from the landscape a few acres so farmers could plant seed and raise grain. If we had been smart we would have left the wetland the way it was and arranged some compromise with farmers. Then the melting snow and the rainfall would have been retained. But it was greed, and our stupidity mixed with poor judgment, because we had had no experience with the consequences.

"Even today we have some departments that are determined to start a far-reaching system of draining-off canals that will stretch hundreds of miles to hundreds of lakes and thousands of marshes and swamps, all to be drained. When we interfered with nature and destroyed the landscape, then our environment struck back with tremendous power.

"Just look at the yearly floods. Where the landscape is drained there is nothing to hold and store the melting snow or downpour. It drains into the ditches, floods the trenches, pours through the canals and rolls into the tributaries. From there on, into the mighty rivers at flood stage. Here we have the same thing year after year, floods and more floods. Villages and towns downstream, big and small, brace themselves against the sweeping surge of the river. Like an avalanche it roars through the landscape. Often it breaks the constructed dikes or sand-sack retaining walls. If that happens, it floods miles of farmland, sweeps into houses and often tears the buildings from their foundations, and carries the houses along.

"Some town folk work night and day building retaining walls against the rising flood. Every year those dikes must be built higher because the river carries along thousands of tons of silt and mud and clay. It then settles in the river bottom, raising the water level year by year. It is really a curse against mankind for his stupidity through the years. Finally there is no other way but to construct a high, mighty dam to control the floodwater. And to do that, we must flood miles of productive farmland. You see we have wrested from the landscape acres for farmers to seed and raise crops, but now we have to flood thousands and thousands of acres of rich farmland for the huge dam's backwater.

"Moreover, we must not forget the pollution of our lakes and streams by ditches and dikes skirting hundreds of farmyards, pig pens, cow pastures and corrals. Every time it rains it washes the dirt into the ditches and from there to lakes and rivers. It is no wonder that our streams and lakes are polluted and stink.

"If the citizens of this great state would look and listen to nature's simple rules and laws, we might still have time to stem the tide. But if we, in our stupidity, purposely dig channels and ditches, then in a few years we might have drought years and dust storms raging our land as in the 1930s."

Now Irvin has picked up a magazine, "The Volunteer" a publication of the Minnesota Department of Conservation. According to this magazine, Minnesota has 214,000 acres of wetland saved. Of course it seems impressive. But the figure must be contrasted with over 10,000,000 acres, the approximate acreage of wetland drained by 50,000 miles of ditches in Minnesota.

In this country we have many private organizations interested and determined to guard and improve our environment, such as Wetlands for Wildlife. Their members have done an excellent job to save many marshes, swamps and potholes on the wide prairies. These clubs' earnest goal is to make it possible again for our wildlife to live and roam again over the landscape as in by-gone years.

The Izaak Walton League of America is another strong organization with branches all over the United States. Its biggest achievement in the Upper Midwest was the sponsorship of legislation to successfully establish the Upper Mississippi Wildlife and Fish Refuge. It was a big undertaking, attacking the river's many environmental ills, such as industrial smokestacks, automobile exhaust, landfills, silation, municipal wastes and landscape pollution, and many more tragic ills that must be corrected in the near future.

The National Audubon Society with its affiliated clubs all over America is an excellent group of people interested in promoting the natural environment for the dwelling and life of our often mistreated birds and animals. Unafraid and proud, they stand eager to promote big undertakings for the welfare of our wildlife. The extraordinarily beautiful magazine, "Audubon" is a "must" for all wildlife friends.

And there is the wonderful magazine, "The National Wildlife," published by the National Wildlife Federation, containing fascinating editorials, many excellent pictures of lakes, rivers and mountains, and of course, some marvelous motifs from the wildlife itself, birds and animals. That magazine has spread its wings over many lands and oceans and is always a stout defender of our American heritage.

Then there is the Sierra Club, founded in 1892 by that great and noble man, John Muir. It carried on its mighty battle for conservation for many years in California, for the Sierra Nevada Mountains, the Yosemite Valley, for the redwoods, and with chapters in many states. It is growing tremendously in numbers every year. It is a mighty political force in the country.

Of course, we have many other fine wildlife organizations worthy of these excellent accomplishments and devoted to this same great purpose. And one is comforted to think that if all these wildlife organizations could form a natural resources league, with its millions of members determined to fight for our precious environment, the future for all of us, mankind and animals, will be safe.

The next morning Max was ready to leave Irvin's attractive place but so many thoughts wandered through his mind. "Enormous is the land. Wonderful are the people. But it has also drawbacks, trouble, turmoil."

Max stood for a long time on the bus station pier looking at two men in a canoe, paddling the long, smooth craft over the enormous lake. Big Bill was in front and Irvin in the back—Irvin, the wilderness professor, now on the first leg of a 500-mile journey, inspecting and looking after things, because when he is called to Washington, D.C., to testify against the wilderness spoilers, he can always say, "I was there. I saw it."

The Dinner

One Sunday after Max had returned from Orvik's Island, he and Heidi were invited to Mr. and Mrs. Grey's home for a venison dinner and to become acquainted with their many friends.

It was a nice Sunday afternoon when they arrived. Mr. Grey was busy out in the patio dressed in a chef's uniform with apron, big gloves and a white cap. The grilled steaks were sizzling, and on a table close by a case of beer was standing. All were asked to help themselves to beer. It was a gay, festive gathering and Max, of course, was the kingpin of the party, and in grand humor. He skoaled with everybody and sometimes, when he talked too fast, it came out half German and half English. But they all understood.

After some time the steak was ready and everybody was handed a plate with a sizzling steak on it and a stein of beer, of course. The table in the dining room was beautifully decorated with flowers and autumn leaves in glorious colors.

The steak was broiled to perfection and all complimented George Grey on being an excellent cook. Max was placed at the head of the table as the honored guest, and soon he lifted his glass to George, the mighty hunter who had wandered out in the deep, dark wood and shot the magnificent buck with his rifle. Each one lifted his glass in a toast to George. However, Mrs. Grey, so proud of her husband's hunting triumph, explained that George did not shoot the buck with a gun but had used a bow and arrow.

Again some of the guests raised their glasses in a salute to George, but Max did not understand what Mrs. Grey had been saying, and he asked if she would please repeat it. Now Mrs. Grey stood up and with a proud gesture, pretended to hold a bow in one hand and pull the bowstring and let the arrow fly with the other hand. Max looked very confused, his sharp, clear eyes wandering from one person to the other. His face turned very red. He finally looked George Grey in the eye and asked if he did not have a rifle to use when he went deer hunting. Yes, George had a whole cabinet full of guns but he loved to go deer hunting with a bow and arrow because it was so fascinating, such a thrill!

Max had been very busy cutting and eating his steak but then he stopped, put his fork and knife slowly on the table. Then in a harsh, suppressed way, he asked if it were a common practice in Minnesota to hunt with a bow and arrow. One of the guests explained that there must be twenty thousand bow-and-arrow hunters every year. Suddenly the room was utterly quiet. Nobody was eating. They all felt that a storm was brewing and they sat looking at Max. Then he said that he could not understand what justification hunters had to shoot deer with a bow and arrow when they had excellent guns and ammunition at home. "And furthermore, I do not understand the conduct of the authorities—allowing hunters to use such barbarous, cruel, and unnecessary ways to harvest their game. It is no wonder that Americans have such a hard time to restore their wildlife when they are so careless, so cruelly heedless in dealing with their fellow creatures on this earth. Would it not be the civilized way to be sure that death came instantly, as quickly, as painlessly as possible?" Max pushed his chair back, stood up and excused himself—fumbling in his pocket for his pipe and tobacco—then walked out to the patio.

It was deathly quiet around the table for some time. Then somebody said that he could not understand why a hunter could not choose his own weapon. Others thought it was very rude of Max to bring this subject up. Now it happened that George Grey's youngest boy had been listening to the talk about the bow and arrow that killed the buck, and he had saved the arrow. He brought it in and put the arrowhead on the table and everybody stared at the hideous thing, full of dried blood and with some meat, torn sinews and hair covering the head of the broken shaft. A silence settled over the gathering. They were all thinking about the deer, cruelly torn and gored by the horrible-looking arrowhead.

George Grey was a well-known person in the community, a soft-spoken and kind-hearted man. Max's protest had been an astonishing shock to him and his face turned red, for he was having painful thoughts about it. Suddenly it struck him with great force—that Max was absolutely right. "We in this country seemed to have no feeling or sympathy for our wild animals and birds. It must be an old habit that we have inherited from the past. We don't see the beautiful creature as a living thing. It is more like a chunk of meat, something to kill and consume. We always believe that we alone have the right to a big happy place on this earth and that animals and birds are put there for us to kill and destroy. From now on I am through hunting in any form. Now I will help to restore our friends, the wild animals, and the sooner the better."

George's feeling flashed in his eyes so earnestly that his guests knew how terribly sincere he was. Many of them, from that time, began to share his feeling.

The coffee and cake and cookies were served in the living room and there Max and George had a long and interesting talk. And when Max left, they sealed a friendship that would last for many years.

Max was looking forward to the opening of deer season, not because he was interested in killing some animals, but he liked to see the size of the deer and the health of the herd.

He found a service station on an intersection of two highways, where he saw the hunters coming back, and many stopped for gas. The owner of the gas station, Gust Malm, was a very likable fellow, always in good humor. A few cars passed up the service station, but a pick-up truck with two deer stopped in for gas. Max was very impressed with those two bucks. They had been in excellent health, for they had shiny coats. He estimated the weight at 230 pounds per buck, and if those animals were an example of the deer herd, then the game department should be very proud of their wildlife. However, his jubilation did not last very long, because the next car had three deer in a trailer. Max looked at the deer in disbelief . . . they were does, and he could see that they had borne calves last spring . . . it must be a mistake! How could anybody kill a doe with some young ones tagging along. For Max, it certainly was a great shock, and it did not take him long to look up Gust, who was having a cup of coffee in the nextdoor restaurant. Max reported to him what he had seen, and asked Gust to call the game warden. Gust shook his head, and informed him that he was not in Germany now. Here in this country, they will kill anything . . . bucks . . . does . . . and even 7 to 8-month-old calves which are only skin and bones . . . hardly worth dragging home. Gust asked Max to sit down and have a cup of coffee. "I will explain the situation to you, Max. It seems we like to get rid of the whole deer herd in a hurry—then it will be less work and worry, and no trouble. This way, if we kill the doe, then the calves will be left alone, and it would be a miracle if the one or two calves born in the spring could live through the severe winter storm, with deep snow, cold weather, with nothing to protect them and lead them to food and shelter. Besides, they are an easy prey for all those wolf packs that search through the wilderness. So, you understand that instead of killing one animal, we get rid of maybe three."

Max was sitting, looking through the window, in deep thought. His face reflected a sad and disappointed expression. He was also wondering if this was the land he had seen and loved as a young boy, and always longed to come back to some day.

He was saying good-bye to Gust, and thanking him for his hospitality. He was going now; he had seen enough.

It had been the understanding that Max would stay with Heidi through the winter, but suddenly, he decided to go back to Germany — to his home. For Heidi, and so many of his new-found friends, it was a big disappointment. But she also had noticed that Max was a changed man, especially after the George Grey dinner, and of course for him to see the slaughtering of the doe, with small ones, was a big shock. Often she found him sitting, pondering. His good humor was a thing of the past, and also when he walked, his steps were shorter and he was not as erect as he used to be.

At the airport, many of his new-found friends regretted that he was going back so soon. George Grey thanked Max for his good advice and suggestions about conservation, and George expressed his thoughts that maybe someday we might have learned to value and appreciate our wildlife. Then, maybe we can tell the rest of the world the civilized way to care for our fauna. Of course, our hope and trust is with the younger generation. They must break new trails in conservation and recognize our failures and the shortsightedness in our saga of our land.

THE BROOK TROUT

The Thomas D. Murphy Company

Nature's Wonderland

The funeral procession of automobiles, forming a long line with headlights turned on, rolled slowly through the city streets and out toward the graveyard on the lake shore. This cemetery was the last resting place of many of the town's wealthy people. At the gate an automobile was waiting and the driver, leading the procession, followed the route winding into the cemetery between trees and shrubs and well-kept lawns to a high knoll with a view of the lake.

This was the last resting place for a man with a good name, well known in the big city and in the state. Norman Brenton had throughout his life gathered wealth and fortune. In his later years he was like a strong vibrating steel spring ready to leap. He was a restless man, always on the go; his enterprises were many and large. He was the head of a huge flourishing company.

One November evening after dark, he had visited one of his farms just a few miles outside the city. On his way home he turned onto a gravel road that followed the section line—a straight road ahead, but with a sharp turn at the end of the section. A big jackrabbit leaped in front of the car, running in the bright automobile lights. He was a fast and powerful runner. With his ears lying straight back on his neck and his head outstretched, the rabbit leaped forward, leap after leap. It looked as though his feet never touched the road. He seemed to float in the air in front of the automobile. The driver gripped the steering wheel with both hands, gazing at the fast-running animal. He wanted to see how fast the rabbit could run.

The driver glanced down at the speedometer—40, 45, and 50 miles per hour. At 60 he was gaining on the animal. His intention was not to kill the rabbit, but just to see how fast he could run. The driver looked up from the speedometer and saw a sharp turn in the road. He slammed on the brakes and the tires shrieked. The car slid from one side of the road to the other. He could not slow down and a big oak tree took the full force of the crash. Glass, steel and metal were in a twisted pile at the roots of the old tree. Some steam from the cracked motor poured out, a gurgling noise from a broken gas tank. That's all. Then it was quiet again, as before, in the peaceful country. On a dusty gravel road lay a dead jackrabbit, and inside a smashed automobile the mutilated body of Norman Brenton.

It was a cold and gray November day at the cemetery. The wind from the lake came sweeping over the final resting place of the well-known man. A sea of flowers from relatives, friends and acquaintances; small and big bouquets in all colors lay side by side in the cold November wind.

There were a great many people huddled around the grave, but there was not room for everyone on the round knoll; some stood on the flat lawn below. In a chair in the front row sat Mrs. Brenton. A hand with a white handkerchief reached under the black veil and wiped away a tear. The young man beside her was Alf Brenton, her only son, her only child. He looked pale and fragile. It looked as though a strong gust of wind would blow him out of the graveyard.

The minister's voice was low. In his hand he held a crushed white rose, the petals of the flower drifting down on the casket; "From earth to earth . . ."

Three days later, early in the morning, Alf Brenton stood in his father's office, alone and feeling like a stranger. Papers and opened letters were stacked high on the wide desk. There were some paintings and pictures on the walls and also a huge map with many pinpointed places where factories, manufacturing companies, farms, flour mills and grain elevators were located. He now owned a great enterprise, but he did not know how to run it. It seemed incredible that in his twenty-nine years of life he had visited the office less than half a dozen times.

He recalled how generous and helpful his dad had been. Many a time his father had asked him to come down to the office . . . anxious to show him around . . . trying hard to kindle a flame that might spread and catch his interest. Maybe at some future time Alf could help him handle the heavy load.

For Alf it had been schools and more schools that were not finished, colleges and universities with no diploma for him, and, of course, lots of traveling. He was always his mother's boy, a kid that never seemed to grow up. He could never play games like other young people—he might be hurt or crippled. His lot was to sit in the grandstand and see the game, see the other boys play. "Don't walk or run or hike. The automobile will take you where you want to go. Be a nice boy. Stay at home, read, or play the piano and go with your mother." That was the advice he received. She was an immovable stone wall between Alf and his dad, jealous and afraid that Alf would take a liking to his father.

When Alf was four years old he had long, curly hair hanging down; he looked like a girl. Once when his dad came home from a long trip, he grabbed the kid, put him into the car and took him to the barber for a haircut. As a result, the mother pretended to get very sick, and went to bed and stayed there for days. After that, Mr. Brenton considered the situation almost hopeless.

Some years later, Mrs. Benton stumbled, sprained her ankle badly and was hospitalized for a long period. It was at this time that Mr. Brenton decided to take a vacation, go north and take the fourteen-year-old boy with him. For Alf, it turned out to be a trip that he never forgot.

After six hours of driving, they hit a road that took them to the landing in the depths of the wilderness. The road was narrow with many curves up hill and down, across narrow bridges, over rivers and creeks, and then at last the landing! That was the end of the road. From there on it was the wilderness, a strange place the astonished boy never knew existed.

At the landing, Alf met Erik Torbu, a a young Norwegian engineer, who after only three years had become Norman Brenton's right-hand man. Mr. Brenton, on a business trip to Germany, had met Erik in a manufacturing plant where Erik had made great progress in a short time. After some correspondence and a generous offer, Erik accepted; he had always wanted to come to America.

Soon all of the camping gear, food and clothing was transferred to the canoe, and they were on their way into the deep, beautiful wilderness, Mr. Brenton in front, Alf in the middle and Erik in the stern of the craft. Before they left the landing Erik made sure that there were three paddles in the canoe. That would give Alf a chance to be on the canoe team. He explained the right way to paddle—a solid grip, the paddle dipped into the water and then pulled. It did not work too well at the start; Alf lost the paddle twice, and they had to stop and pick it up. After that Erik took a shoelace from a boot, tied the grip of the paddle to Alf's hand, and from there on things went better.

Alf was in the best of humor, feeling fine, gripping the paddle with all his might. He was on the team where a man is a man and he was one of them.

The day was so warm they stripped to the waist. Erik knew Alf's story but was still surprised to see how poorly developed he was at the age of fourteen. His back, shoulders and arms seemed to have no muscle. How could that selfish woman have been so blind as to not see what was happening to her son? If Erik had his way with Alf, inside of two or three years the boy would have a wonderful physique with bulging muscles; he would be strong and have lots of stamina.

After some time Erik noticed that the boy was getting tired, so they decided to have lunch and rest on one of the small islands. For Alf it was a wonderful new experience. Soon the fire was going, the coffee was boiling and the bacon and eggs were sizzling in the pan. He felt hungry, which was something new for him. He had always been a finicky eater, never asking for a second helping. His soft hands had developed blisters from paddling the canoe. Erik noticed that the blisters were bothering Alf, but to tell him that he could not paddle any more would put a damper on his good humor and he might resent it.

After lunch Erik spread out a map of the wilderness and taught Alf to read it and also to navigate by compass. When they started out again, Alf felt very important, sitting there directing the course they were to take. They entered the main canoe route and met others paddling their craft, smiling, laughing and waving with friendly greetings. They were suntanned and healthy. As they entered the narrows where several men were fishing, Mr. Brenton and Erik inquired about the fishing luck. Some of the fishermen shook their heads, others lifted a nice catch of fish out of the water.

Farther on where the current was strong they found a capsized canoe with three girls trying hard to right the craft, which was almost impossible in the swift current. The men pulled their canoe alongside, lifted the girls aboard, and then towed the overturned canoe to shallow water. A big boulder in the narrows had tipped the girls' canoe and dumped the whole load into the stream. Erik, who was an excellent swimmer, retrieved most of the girls' belongings and also found many things that did not belong to the girls. Somebody else evidently had the same tough luck at this spot. In due time most of the equipment was recovered, even some of the food, but, of course, it was water-soaked. The girls made camp on a small island not far from the main shore to dry their sleeping bags, blankets and clothing. The menfolk crossed the narrows to the mainland.

After the girls dried their clothing, Erik invited them to supper. The food tasted wonderful out in the fresh air. After supper they all sat around a cheery campfire, talking, singing and telling stories. How interesting, how fascinating for Alf! One of the girls, named Caroline, a laughing, charming person with a fine voice, sang *Indian Love Call, Pale Moon* and *By the Waters of Minnetonka*. The songs were very fitting for this occasion. The notes drifted out over the deep blue lake with dark shadows toward the shoreline.

After the songs, Caroline sat down. Nobody said anything. The wilderness mood had grasped their dreams in mysterious harmony with something they all had longed for.

Later the girls returned to their own camp. The men also retired. Alf decided he wanted to sleep outside under the stars. For the first time in his life he felt in harmony with the world—a strange, tranquil feeling of peace in this great unknown region. So many thoughts and new impressions occupied his mind; so many new and interesting things had happened in the short time he had been here. He hoped to get the answers to the many questions he wished to ask. He wondered if all the people he had met and seen that day were from the cities and villages. If so, why were they so changed—so friendly, so helpful and in such good humor—no growling, swearing or bad tempers? But why were they so changed? It might be, as his father told him on their way to the wilderness, "Here all are alike, rich and poor. All own a share of the wonderful land. The wilderness belongs to everyone in this great nation, every citizen, young and old. Outside of this territory one might have millions of dollars in property and wealth, be a big industrialist, a great banker or landowner, but here in the wilderness all are alike. Most of the people rent their canoes, some rent their equipment, some own it. It makes very little difference. There is no luxury liner, no high-speed boat, no outboard motor—they all paddle their canoes in a happy and wonderful world. They forget the everyday grind and nerve-wracking life with its worry and strain. They feel free in the new-found land."

Alf, in his sleeping bag, could see many bright stars through the branches of a tall Norway pine. The wilderness' soothing quietness had settled into his mind. His eyes were half closed, dreaming. He could still hear the small waves rolling toward the shore with a soft splash, breaking on the sandy beach, and way out between the many islands and the narrows he heard the rumble of a gushing waterfall tumbling out into the lake. It sounded like a subdued bass drum, a soloist in the wilderness symphony. Sleep and dream, young boy! Mother Nature bids you welcome and the Wilderness has captured you!

The next morning at sunrise, Mr. Brenton and Erik went fishing in the narrows and returned with a nice catch of northern pike, enough for a couple of days. When they reached camp, Alf was still sound asleep with his arms outside the sleeping bag. Erik, with a sympathetic look, noticed the thin arms and neck, like those of a scrawny chicken with the feathers plucked off.

Soon they had a good fire going and fish frying in the pan. Mr. Brenton, with good humor, banged on a kettle and hollered over to the girls: "Come and get it." Alf awakened and stretched himself. It was a new day for him. He had something to look forward to. Life was wonderful! In no place in the world did food taste so good as in the wilds.

The men had checked their food supply, and when the girls were ready to leave, gave them enough food to last until a new supply of provisions could be purchased. As some of the girls' camping equipment were still hanging wet in the sun the girls decided not to start out immediately. As the men left camp heading north, the girls waved good-bye to their new-found friends of the wilderness — two men and a boy, happy to be exploring the unknown.

The canoe trip of a few days was a new discovery for Alf. For him, every half hour brought something new, to walk on the soft moss-covered ground, or to picnic beside a small, tumbling, laughing waterfall. For the first time in his life, he was looking forward to a new day. The only thing that really bothered Alf was that is was so hard for him to breathe deeply. He finally asked Erik about it and Erik explained that his lungs were not used to this wonderful fresh air, "Because the air in the wilderness is almost like pure oxygen. It is not like the polluted city air, full of smoke, dust, and dirt, not to mention the exhaust fumes from cars, trucks and buses.

"It seems incredible," said Erik, "that on all these motor-driven vehicles, we have air-cleaners where the air enters the motor and is filtered through an oil bath. That's for the motors. But for the human beings, we don't have any external air-cleaner to filter the air we breathe. It seems that we are more concerned with our motors than with human lives."

The men stayed an extra day at Alf's request. For him, it was so hard to leave this wonderful life.

And then came the return trip. It was not a welcome party for Mr. Brenton and Alf when they reached home. Mr. Brenton was lucky. He did not have time to listen to this raving madwoman, Mrs. Brenton, but for Alf it was a different story. For a while, Alf put up a good front. Soon however, tears of self-pity from his mother broke down all his resistance and he was back in the old rut—like a puppy tagging along with his mother. He dreamed often about the canoe trip in the wilderness. Sometimes it seemed so real. He could still hear Caroline's warm voice and the echo from *By the Waters of Minnetonka* floating from island to island until finally the notes died out in the west, in the sunset on the still fjord.

* * *

Though the canoe trip happened fifteen years ago, Alf could not understand where the time went. It had been thoroughly wasted. He could not remember a single project, a single accomplishment that he had achieved. How could anybody be so blind to all the things that went on and how could he have accomplished so little?

The accident that killed his dad was a severe blow to him. It seemed that everything crumbled and fell. Now, as he sat in the big office in his dad's chair, he felt like a lost soul. He thought: "What is the next important thing to do? Where do I start? How can I make any essential decisions?"

If only he could live the last fifteen years over again! Miss Morris, his dad's private secretary, knocked on the door of the office and greeted Alf with a friendly smile and a warm welcome. Miss Morris was not new in her position. She had been with the Brenton Company for many years, and had great knowledge and experience in her work. Mr. Brenton always used to say: "The Brenton Company could never run without Miss Morris."

Since the funeral, she had had plenty of time to think things over. She decided that the best thing for Alf would be if she continued to arrange matters, just as she did when Mr. Brenton was the president. She knew that Alf was in a bad situation, with no knowledge at all about the company. So she told him that she had called in all the superintendents of the eight plants to attend a meeting in his office at ten o'clock on Wednesday morning. They all replied that they would be present. She had a long list of appointments for Alf, papers to be signed by him and also important decisions for him to make. She had asked Erik to come and told Alf, "He will be here in a short time and generally he is well informed about all company affairs."

It had been Alf's intention to sell the Brenton Company as soon as possible; but after the meeting with the superintendents and listening to their opinions, he decided that he was in no hurry to sell. He also remembered that his dad had told him, "You know there is not only your interest to consider, but also that of all those thousands of workers who depend on you."

As for Mrs. Brenton, Alf's mother, she certainly had great plans in store for Alf and herself. After they had sold their enterprises, they would travel all over the world and have a great time—visit foreign countries and meet dazzling, important people.

But her dream came to an abrupt end. The holdings were not to be sold; and furthermore, Alf was now going to work in earnest and learn to manage those huge plants himself. To start with, she absolutely refused to believe it! Impossible! But it took only a few days for Alf to change from a wretch of a kid to a man with his own opinions. There were many scenes with tears, begging and finally raging anger, before his mother came to the conclusion that Alf was firm in his decision and that he was not a little boy anymore. Well! She certainly was not going to spend her whole life sitting, fading away, in this dull city!

Alf, as the president of the huge Brenton Company, soon discovered that it was no small matter to run big enterprises. Even with the immense helpfulness of Miss Morris and Erik, it was a frightening task. Now he understood what a great job his father had done through the many years, and groaned to think how he had been of no assistance to his dad. After the first two months, the company showed a healthy profit and nobody was thinking in terms of selling. It seemed that everyone was concerned about Alf's health, especially Miss Morris and Erik. Finally, they persuaded him to see a doctor for a check-up. A thorough check in a clinic revealed that Alf's heart was not very strong, and that someday it might fail. He would in the future have to be extremely careful not to overwork. The report seemed to make an impression on him for a while, but after a few weeks he was back at the same reckless pace.

* * *

Then spring came and with it the first warm day in the new year. Alf planned to take the weekend off—just to rest and take it easy. He was sitting in the barber chair having a haircut. It felt so good to sit down after a rough week. He had experienced some pain in his chest of late, but paid no attention to it as it always disappeared after a while, but he could not understand those sharp pains like needles in his arms. That was something new to him, but when his arm and hand started to get numb, accompanied by a wild pounding of his heart, he knew what had happened.

The next thing he knew he was in the hospital flat on his back. The best heart specialist was called in and after a thorough examination all agreed that the heart seizure was not too serious but that he must be very careful for a long time.

It so happened that Dr. Stein, one of the best heart specialists in the country, was on a tour through the state and found Alf an interesting case. Dr. Stein, who was not a young man by any means, was full of energy and showed delightful good humor. He explained to Alf that he was not alone in his dilemma: "We have thousands and thousands of young men in the same boat. The heart is a muscle, a wonderful contraption and with healthy exercise, hard work, walking, hiking and participating in sports, a person can develop his heart until it is strong. The main thing is to start young and never let up. A sound mind in a sound body should be the goal for everybody."

"Excuse the sermon," said Dr. Stein, smiling. And he explained to Alf how his heart was like a soft, slack, flimsy muscle. "Then when you work too hard and put too much strain on it, your heart cannot take it. Many of our fine young men die of heart attacks even before they reach their prime of life. Too many people live in a push-button world; it takes no strength to push a button or to pull a lever."

The result was that Erik was appointed top man in the Brenton Company, which seemed to work out satisfactorily.

* * *

One day in midsummer, with its long, light days and short nights, Alf was home, just lying around, feeling downhearted and out of sorts. He had been daydreaming and could not put a certain idea from his thoughts; it always came back stronger than before. Miss Morris and Erik were having dinner with Alf that day when he let them in on his thoughts. He wanted to go to the wilderness again! If he had to recuperate much longer, he would die of boredom. "And so my mind is made up," he said, "If I am going to die, it can just as well be in the wilderness."

Miss Morris looked flabbergasted. She couldn't understand it. He wanted to go to that wild country where there were no drugs, no hospitals, no decent accommodations! She was sure that he would not live a month! Perhaps not even a week!

They were both looking at Erik. So much depended on his opinion. If he sided with Miss Morris, then Alf knew that his idea would remain a dream, a fantasy. Erik sat with a smile on his face. Then presently he looked at Alf and asked: "How come it took you so long to decide to go? Your cabin on Kvanro Lake has been ready and waiting for two weeks!"

Alf beamed all over, "Erik! Hurrah! Thank you for saying it! Now I can start living again!"

The cabin on Kvanro Lake belonged to a widow by the name of Mrs. Lindle. It had been standing empty for two years, since her husband died. She had planned to put it up for sale, but Erik persuaded her to let Alf have first chance. The cabin was a beauty, standing on a point on Kvanro Lake, surrounded by 8,000 acres of forest, lakes and streams. The lake, which also belonged to Mrs. Lindle, was not in the primitive wilderness, but Kvanro Lake joined Skagan Lake, which did belong to the canoe area.

"The cabin," said Erik, "is modern, with telephone, radio, television, and the road to the cabin is wide and easy to drive on. It seems to be perfect for you, Alf."

Alf and Erik anxiously invited Miss Morris to go along for the weekend, but she absolutely refused. The idea! What would she do up in this God-forsaken country, with swamps, rocks and mountains, not to mention all those thousands of mosquitoes? "Bugs and bees! No thank you!" She had her apartment and if she wanted to see trees, there was a nice park in town.

Alf was so excited about the trip. It would be just two more days. They would leave by noon on Friday and reach the cabin by 5 o'clock. What a life! He could hardly wait! It was many long and useless years since he had been in that unforgettable wilderness with his dad and Erik.

The day was warm and sticky when Miss Morris came back to her apartment after dinner with Alf and Erik. The air in the room was hot and humid, with the sun pouring through the windows. She pulled the curtains and changed her clothes. She could not get Alf and Erik out of her mind, for she did not understand why they were so crazy about a cabin in the wilderness. She could not forget Alf's look when Erik told him about the cabin. He was just like a boy receiving a wonderful Christmas gift! It certainly aroused her curiosity. She couldn't understand why the wilderness was such a grand place. "Those guys must be crazy. If there were gold and diamonds to be found there it would be a different story; but to go just to look at swamps, lakes and trees—well, those things people can see just outside the city."

She poured herself a drink, lit a cigarette, and sat down in an easy chair and let her thoughts wander back over the past few years. She was thirty-three and had not had much adventure in her life. Work.

Going to church. Occasional parties. Night clubs and beer taverns. Of course she had dates, going out with fellows. Life had not been too exciting.

She looked over her apartment. It would soon be ten years since she had moved there. Well, it was nothing to brag about. "Same thing day after day. I certainly have been in a rut for a long time."

She looked at the cigarette in disgust and squashed it in an ash tray. She took another sip of the drink and poured the remainder in the sink.

"I am going with the boys to the cabin in the wilderness if it kills me!"

It was Friday at high noon. Two cars were heading north on the wide superhighway. Erik led the way and Alf was in the second car with Miss Morris as driver. North, north! They passed beautiful farms, lakes and rivers—hills where the oak trees stood thick and tall—then the evergreen trees took over, Norway pines, spruce, fir and balsam.

After some hours they left the superhighway and turned into a secondary road. The farms here were smaller and often only a clearing in the forest. After some time a big sign appeared, "Lindle Estate." Those woods belonged to the Lindles. Only a couple more miles and they were at the cabin. At the entrance gate stood two tall men dressed in Scottish costumes, kilts and carrying bagpipes and drums. The men let Erik's car pass, but they walked ahead of Alf and Miss Morris' car with a fast-stepping march and blaring bagpipes. When these martial Scots reached the cabin, they quit playing.

Alf and Miss Morris were introduced to Bruce Sinclair, his wife, Orun, and his son, Stuart. A more glorious welcome was never bestowed on royalty.

The cabin, built of thick, heavy logs, was large but cozy, with large plate glass windows looking out on the lake. In the living room on the long wall was a big fireplace built in Scandinavian style. Around the fireplace were chairs made of huge logs but lined with thick upholstery inside and beautifully hand carved outside. There were three bedrooms besides the sleeping porch. It was a cabin fit for a king.

On the screen-porch was a round table already set with old silver and fine glassware; and on a big platter lay a broiled fresh fish from the deep, crystalline lake. It was a festive party, the dinner was excellent and Miss Morris, who had been a little tense and anxious, was in grand humor. She felt so at home. Forgotten was the prosaic life of every day—the gloomy atmosphere, the steady strain, the ruthless economic battle. She even suggested that everybody call her by her first name, Kari.

Bruce Sinclair asked her to go fishing, a thing she had never done. Bruce decided to take a sturdy boat instead of a canoe so Kari would feel more secure. Never would she forget the thrill of sitting there with the fishing rod and feeling the first nibble at the bait. Then came the solid strike. She got so excited she screamed and Bruce had to help her land the fish. And that was not the only one she got. After some time they were rowing toward shore. She was not an expert with the oars, but she learned fast.

The next morning the dawn was breaking! It was the start of a new day on Kvanro Lake. The first golden beams of the rising sun flickered on the steel gray heavens. Some light blue flames, shimmering, blended with the dark blue of the night and soon it was a brilliant blue. Welcome to the new day! Kari had never seen a sunrise in the wilderness, only in town where the sun rose over the house roofs. She stood spellbound as the warm, golden arch rose in the east. The arch grew in length and height. The first glow was peeking over the horizon.

Then from the lake came long and loud laughter; then another burst of it. How could people be so noisy in such splendor? It must be some city folks who don't know any better. It certainly was a shame to awaken all the people around the lake so early; and she was going to put a stop to it. A few minutes later she was ready. As she pushed the boat out from the shore, she had a little trouble. The boat dragged on the sand, so she slipped off her shoes and stockings, stepped into the water, pushed the boat from the shore, and was on her way.

The whole lake was still and clear, just like a mirror; some light clouds drifted overhead. It seemed as if they were floating on the crystal clear water — like a noiseless dream. She took a few strokes with the oars. The boat and the oars made small ripples on the lake and somehow she felt that it was not right to disturb the peaceful fjord.

She had made up her mind, however, that she wanted to find out about the people who were so rudely disturbing the wonderful morning. She thought the laughter had come from a small island not too far away. It took her some time to get there. When she got closer to the island, resting on the oars she searched the shoreline for people but could not see anybody. So she rowed toward the other side of the island. But there was not a living soul! As she came around a sharp point, a big black bird with some white stripes took off in fast flight, and it laughed so loudly it could be heard all over the lake.

Kari sat there astonished. How stupid of her! She should have known that it was a loon that made such wonderful laughter. He was the life of the party in the wilderness! It was a good thing that the men were not up yet. If they knew what she had done, they certainly would have had a good time teasing her.

She decided to row back to the mainland and follow the shoreline northward. As she rounded a point, there, in a clearing on the lake shore, stood an old church, weatherbeaten by sun and rain through many years. She pulled the boat onto the shore and walked to the old, forsaken, lonely church through an open gate. There was a high, thick, stone wall on all sides, enclosing the cemetery, with wooden crosses standing on sunken, forgotten graves. One could still make out names on many of the markers, folks who had lived and died in their struggle to wrestle from the sandy soil a scant living.

The graves were utterly forlorn. Thick grass grew over them but with many wild flowers. The pathos and poetry of it struck her. These people were born and raised here. They preferred the peaceful forest with struggle and sacrifice to the town's noise and rumble with its nervous life. She looked at the stones in the huge wall all around the cemetery, those thousands and thousands of big and small cobblestones piled on top of each other! It must have been a gigantic task to gather all of them. The workmen must have been strong and muscular, their backs bent from many years of hard work.

Then came, she thought, the second generation with a different slant on life. They moved toward an easier, safer living. The church and the graves were soon forgotten, and also the good souls that rested in the peaceful forest.

She pushed the church door. It squeaked on the hinges as it swung open and she walked in. The room was quite dark. The windows were swathed in thick cobwebs, which hung down and covered the small frames. Here in the quietness, the saga of the past streamed through—people's hope, struggle and deep love for the forest. Sometime long ago, she imagined, talk and laughter had rung out, especially from the young ones. On the wall above the altar hung a wooden cross, rugged and rough, with marks visible from a distance. Through a small dirty window a pale sunbeam flickered over the cross, which was brown in color, with wide, long cracks in the cross beams. The altar cloth was still there, but faded and torn.

Kari brushed the dust from a wooden bench and sat down. She began thinking that it would be a wonderful thing to restore the old church and graveyard. Yes, she would make it her project. It would be like the old hymn, "Come to the Church in the Wildwood." She would re-create it carefully so as not to destroy its old charm. Bells could be installed in the small tower, and in summer the bells would ring out over the wilderness and the lake. People from far and wide would come for Sunday services. Suddenly, Kari felt that she had a purpose in life, something to do that was worthwhile.

At breakfast that same morning, Kari's spirit and her idea about the old church inspired the others. They all agreed that it would be a great project and that it should be started as soon as possible. After breakfast all five were on their way to inspect the old church, Kari, Alf and Bruce in the boat, with Stuart and Erik hiking the small trail. They met inside the gate at the cemetery.

They talked in low voices. Here the silently passing and vanishing years whispered in living memory of families that had lived and died in this peaceful forest, buried and forgotten! New generations were born. They went away. And the old church faded into oblivion.

They inspected the church inside and out. It would be a big project they all agreed, but it certainly would be wonderful to save such a jewel.

Monday morning at five o'clock, Kari and Erik were on their way back home to their jobs. Kari stopped at her apartment, opened the door and stood there looking. It had always seemed to be so big, roomy and neat. Now it looked so tiny. It seemed as though the walls were squeezed in. She suffered with a feeling that the room was too small and that she must push the walls back. She could not understand what had happened.

In the evening when Erik was ready to leave the office, Kari said, "Well, it's one down and three and a half to go." Erik stood there for a minute. Yes, three and a half days! Friday noon, we shall be on our way north. The wilderness is calling!

When Erik and Kari left the cabin on Kvanro Lake early on Monday morning, the rest were sound asleep. The discussion that had followed the visit to the forlorn and forgotten little church had lasted into the late hours.

* * *

At breakfast, Alf, Bruce and his wife planned a program to restore Alf's health. They all agreed that it would not be easy; but from Bruce's own boyhood experience, he knew that it could be done.

Bruce Sinclair, born in Scotland, came to America as a young man. His brother, who owned a grocery store in this country, gave Bruce work in the store. He was at that time very slender, tall, pale and thin. He did not mind working in the store, but he hated more than anything else to be called—no matter how jokingly—Skinny or Bony. He despised those who would call out to him, "Come here, Skinny," or "Hi, Bony!"

One day he met a husky fellow who had fine, considerate manners and never called Bruce "Skinny," but on the other hand, he did not admire thin men. One day he said to young Bruce: "If you are not sick or if there is nothing wrong with you, why don't you improve your appearance? If you will follow my instructions in earnest—it is not going to be easy—I promise that inside of two years, nobody will have the nerve to call you skinny."

Bruce held a conference with his brother, and the latter was more than willing to help out in this program, even to the extent of purchasing the equipment necessary to get Bruce started. This meant dumbbells, many weights of different sizes, ropes and springs. When these implements arrived, there was no way for Bruce to back out. He had to start.

September came and went. Also October, with very little progress. By the middle of November things began to happen. The dumbbells were lifted with more vigor, power and determination. In December came the first snow, a thick layer of the beautiful, white, fluffy stuff. The routine weight lifting was changed to skiing. Bruce had had some experience skiing in the old country. He loved the snow and out-of-doors, the fields and forest, with hills, slopes and meadows. So now he laid out a five-mile ski trail that ran between stumps and stones, over fences, up and down hills, along slopes, and around sharp turns.

The worst part was the steep hills where he sometimes had to walk sideways. He found the herringbone ascent to be much faster after he had experience. Going straight up the hill was the hardest, where he desperately hung on to the ski poles, pushing. It is on the steep hill that the skier develops a wonderful physique with a strong heart and powerful muscles. The fresh air fills the lungs and chest; it brings red blood to the body, red cheeks, sparkling eyes and a rosy complexion.

Bruce was a good-hearted, helpful and easy-going person ordinarily, but the sight of ski-lifts and ski-ropes made his blood boil. When the Norwegians introduced skiing to America, it was a healthy and vigorous sport. To reach the top of the hill the skiers carried their skis on their shoulders or went up the hill on their skis. It was hard going and lots of good exercise. Today, the skier hangs on to a rope and is pulled up the hill or he sits lazily in the lift as he is transported to the hilltop. Skiing has become a lazy man's hobby. It certainly would be a wonderful thing for the millions of skiers in the world today if those unhealthy ski-lifts and ski-ropes could be removed forever. Bruce thought that there should be thousands and thousands of young men and women on the country's cross-country ski runs during the winter. It is a sad thing that so few of our young people have the necessary ambition and love for a good body-building sport such as skiing.

By the following spring Bruce had improved. It was amazing what sport and exercise had done for him. He had a ruddy face, big shoulders and strong, well-muscled legs.

He was given a new job—working for a contractor building houses. He had to handle bricks and cement, sacks and blocks. The hardest job was to push those heavy wheelbarrows full of soft concrete up an incline. The first two weeks he was so tired that he could hardly get home in the evening. And then to start again the next morning! But he never gave up.

After two months it was a different story; he could work with equipment like an old hand. The most important thing for him was that nobody ever called him "Skinny," or "Bony." Those nicknames he had left behind. He was a changed man—full of life and good humor.

A year later, he was back working in the grocery store. His brother had been killed in an automobile accident and Bruce took over the store. Somehow he was not satisfied to be cooped inside, but he had no choice. One day, as he was standing, bent over the store counter looking at some pictures of the lake cabin, he glanced down at the floor in front of him and discovered a pair of shoes, two legs, a blue skirt, a white and red sweater, a bright blue muffler, a smiling face, no make-up, blonde, curly hair and a pair of the bluest eyes he had ever seen. He looked at the groceries she had put on the counter. He rang up the amount on the cash register, received the money, gave her the change and put the groceries in a bag. She picked up the bag, walked toward the door, opened it, turned back and smiled at him—with a giggle.

The moment she had left he started thinking: "So stupid of me, standing there saying nothing! She must think I am deaf!" Then he started wondering what her name was and where she came from.

It was Sunday afternoon in February with bright sunshine, deep snow and an excellent ski-glide on the trail! Bruce was out for cross-country skiing for the first time in the new year. There had not been much snow and his work in the store had been most demanding. He had shortened the ski trail to three miles, so that if he felt like it, he could cover the distance twice. It seemed wonderful to be out in the country again. Snow, so pure and white, covered the landscape, hung on the tree branches; and the air was fresh and invigorating.

Bruce was having a hard time going up a steep hill. When he reached the top he was confronted with a long downgrade where he could pick up speed. He had to be careful, because at the bottom there was a sharp turn. He was sailing right along. Then from behind somebody shouted: "Coming through!" He stepped out of the tracks, wondering who could be skiing so fast. He glanced to the side and there was a girl passing him in a fast spurt as though he were standing still. He intended to warn her about the dangerous turn at the bottom of the hill, but she was already too far away. She would not hear him. He knew that with that speed, she would not be able to make the sharp turn. She would be sliding right into the woods and there would be broken arms and legs. When she was only a short distance from the turn, she put the brakes on, skis spread out in back and in front like a snow plow. She was breaking speed. Snow whirled around her. He could see only the top of her. Then just before she hit the turn she straightened the skis out, made a quick flashing turn, and disappeared.

Bruce was flabbergasted. He had never seen such fine ski form, such perfect technique, such a trailblazer! He remembered that there was a fence some distance ahead. There she would have to take off her skis to crawl over the fence. That would take some time and maybe he could talk to her there.

When he came to the clearing in the woods, she was ahead of him at the fence. She put her ski poles over the fence on the opposite side, and then with one hand grabbing hold of the high fence post and with the other hand further down, she swung herself over with a leap, skis and all! Then she grabbed her ski poles and disappeared.

After this small drama, Bruce was not in a hurry the rest of the way. Just before he reached the starting point, somebody behind him called: "Coming through," and lo and behold, she was passing him again. At the finish line, she stood waiting for him and greeted him with "Hello, Slowpoke!" They both burst out laughing, and he recognized her as the girl he had seen but not talked to in his store.

He introduced himself and she said that her name was Orund Lylja. That was the start of a friendship which was to last through many skiing seasons. Often they took the bus out of town for several miles, where they skied cross-country. When they got tired, they would sit in the snow and have lunch—the hot coffee was delicious beyond words!

They were married the next spring, and a year later Stuart was born, and then Sylvia.

Some twenty years rolled by and a big shopping center bought their store. After this the family moved to Kvanro Lake to enjoy a life they had dreamed about for a long time. As good friends of Erik, they promised to see what they could do for Alf. With Orund's cooking and under Bruce's watchful eye, Alf changed from a thin, gangling youth to a muscular athlete.

* * *

According to Dr. Stein's theory, Bruce and Orund did not consider Alf a sick man, which could have in many ways hindered his progress. The health exercises started with a short morning walk, then rest; in the afternoon there was rowing and swimming. The hikes gradually were longer and faster. The fresh air and sunlight helped him to become healthy and strong.

One day Bruce asked Alf to help him build a bridge over the creek. It had to be strong enough to carry automobiles and small trucks. The timber for the bridge was cut and dragged to the crossing, which gave Alf vigorous exercise. The day Alf started to swing the ax was for Orund and Bruce a sight they would never forget. He swung the ax like a baseball bat and never hit the same cut twice in a row. However, he learned fast and when Erik and Kari came for the weekend, they were quite impressed with his progress.

They all pitched in working. It was not really work; they had so much fun laughing and joking. Here were five people, jovial, happy and in tune with the wilderness!

The bridge was ready in a couple of weeks and the next project planned was the restoration of the church. They trucked the necessary material over the bridge to the church. Their contractor, who was from this northern land, was very much interested and had many years' experience in building log cabins and halls. With plenty of help, it would not be long before the church was ready. Not only had the contractor caught the spirit in restoring the church, but many other local people willingly helped.

It was the last Sunday of September when the church bell rang out in the sparkling autumn air, calling everybody to worship in the restored church. People came from all over, some hiking, some driving, some sailing in canoes. Folks from many denominations and beliefs packed into the old church. They listened to a young preacher give the sermon and ardently sung the hymns played on the old organ. It was the first service there for many, many years.

Afterwards, all the people were invited to the Whispering Pine cabin where Alf and his co-workers served refreshments. All the guests were in good spirits.

In late October, Kvanro Lake froze over. The ice lay thick and smooth over the great fjord. Skating and other winter sports were in full swing. It seemed that so many people came to the Whispering Pine cabin that it often looked like a gala, fashionable resort. For many of the city dwellers, it was a hard thing to leave the cabin in the wilderness, and many of them lingered on for days. On Thanksgiving, there was a big gathering with all joining in the skiing, skating and tobogganing. What a delightful, rollicking time! A new cabin had been added to the building, and also a pretty log house with a Finnish sauna bath in it. A young Finnish woman, who was in charge, kept the stones for steam sizzling hot. Each guest had to go outside after his bath and roll in the fresh snow. And each one was given a quick going over with a whisk broom made of small pliable twigs and branches, smacking the bathers all over their bodies. For many of them it was the most stimulating experience they had ever dreamed of.

But Christmas was the most wonderful time of the year. The spirit caught them all. In the forenoon sheaves of wheat were hung out in the trees and great lumps of suet were put on elevated platforms for the birds. The Yule tree was selected, cut and moved into the living room, its woodland fragrance filling the house. Delightful, intoxicating! Just before noon Erik and Alf put on skis and hiked over to the church in the wilderness. They opened the shutters on the spire and at high noon the chimes rang out over the snow-covered landscape, proclaiming Christmas and Peace on Earth.

When they returned to the cabin, they found the tree was fully decorated and sparkling with lights. After a festive meal they all put on their skis for a hike through the majestic, quiet, winter-white forest where the towering Norway pines stood snow-covered, each one like a king in his white satin and ermine-trimmed robe.

In the evening they sat by a warm and cozy fire, with the two dogs sleeping soundly by the hearth, while at the side the Christmas tree glittered with ruby and emerald lights and golden tinsel. The table was set with old silver, wine glasses and lighted candles. From the kitchen came the smell of roasted turkey. Gifts were exchanged with laughter and exclamations of delight.

Eric took some papers out of his briefcase and gave them to Alf. They were the Torrens title to the Whispering Pines cabin and all its eight thousand acres. In addition, Alf was the owner of an immense wilderness area, nearly as big as a county. What a Christmas it had been!

* * *

Years rolled by. Alf was back at work again and doing a most admirable job. He was the picture of health; broad-shouldered, erect, with a ruddy complexion and a wide smile. He and Sylvia, Bruce and Orund's daughter, were now married. She was a beautiful girl, very athletic and wonderfully pretty with curly, golden hair.

It was not a big wedding, but quite simple and charming, in the old church in the wilderness. In the candlelight above the altar they could see the the old rugged cross, brown in color with its ax marks and cracks. That was just the kind of wedding they wanted, simple and true, like the wilderness itself.

The region had changed. Brenton's Landing, the gateway to the virgin wilderness and canoe area, was now a small town that was growing with leaps and bounds. People moved in and started businesses. One company made canoes for sale and for rent. Some made tents, sleeping bags, sailboats and all kinds of equipment for canoeing and camping. It was a lively town with hotels and motor courts that were always filled, and there were some nice restaurants. Alf started a school where young men could learn to be wilderness guides and wilderness inspectors. An inspector's job was to enforce the laws and regulations in the wilderness.

These men were carefully selected for their friendly and helpful nature, but they also had to be tough and hard when it came to dealing with spoilers, poachers and litterbugs. The inspectors used fast boats and airplanes so they could sweep in on the lawbreakers or offer help to campers in emergencies.

Then there was a large maintenance crew, traveling over the area, repairing camps and building new ones. Before the tourists left Brenton's Landing for the wilderness they had to be posted on the regulations. All firearms were left at the landing, even bows and arrows. Canoe and hiker fees were put back into the operation. Alf and his friends discovered that most travelers were wonderful people. They were true lovers of nature and were anxious to keep the forest undefiled.

Otto Stabur, the game warden in the Kvanro Lake territory for many years, knew the surrounding country better than anyone else. One day in June he came over to the Whispering Pine cabin and informed Alf that in a certain swampy territory in his woods lots of deer were dying from starvation during the long winters. The deer, frightened into the swamp during the hunting season, did not come out until the following spring. They were often so weak, many died on the way out.

The territory was full of swamps, lowland and thick underbrush, so much so that it was practically impossible to hunt deer there and drag the dead animals out. Year after year, more and more deer went into the swamp where there was less and less food for the big herd.

It was a very serious group of people that sat around the breakfast table that Sunday morning. They were appalled at the thought of the starving, dying animals and agreed that something must be done about it before the next winter.

Stuart had a good idea. He suggested that some men be sent there during the summer to make a clearing in the woods for a cabin. A helicopter could transport men and materials in as soon as the clearing was ready. In the fall after the first hard frost, the best man from the game warden's organization would be flown into harvest some of the deer, so the rest would not starve. The deer which were killed would then be dragged to the clearing and onto the ice as soon as it was strong enough for the helicopter to land. The animals would then be flown to the nearest highway where a truck could transport them to the meat-locker and the game warden could sell the venison.

Orund, Kari and Sylvia were against killing those beautiful animals. They insisted that there must be another way to save them. Why not fly some hay in to feed the deer? Otto informed the ladies that it was not quite that simple. A starving deer could lie beside a bale of hay and never touch it. Twigs and branches were its food, not hay. If they could not find the right food they would starve. If the Wildlife Department could find a way to feed those hungry creatures it certainly would be done.

Erik sat for some time thinking. He was wrestling with the problem of teaching the starved deer to eat hay! Their natural food was twigs and brush branches. "Suppose we got a big gang together this summer to harvest twigs and branches and young trees that the deer feed on. The twigs and branches could be gathered in sheaves, banded together, and dropped from an airplane to the starving animals. The first bundles dropped would be only twigs and branches, but the next bundles would have a certain amount of hay mixed in. The deer would eat the hay with the twigs and little by little they would be taught to eat."

That same summer, a group of boys and girls was formed to try out this experiment. Surely those bundles of twigs and branches with leaves still attached would taste wonderful to the starving deer!

And so the next winter, with the first deep snow and cold weather, the first bundles of twigs in sheaves were dropped from a helicopter to the starving animals. The deer scattered in all directions, but soon returned to eat. By afternoon, the bundles had been consumed. The next morning a fresh load of bundles was delivered with some hay added to it. Two weeks later, the deer population was eating like horses. A way had been found to save hundreds of deer from starving to death!

Alf had a generous spirit and was eager to share his worldly goods with other people. His next project was to restore the old CCC camps so that boys from the cities could have the opportunity to work in the healthy out-of-doors—building cabins, clearing woods, constructing camps and making trails in the wilderness. There would also be camps for girls and outdoor projects for them. Someday these young folks would be the leaders of our country, outstanding citizens of a great land.

BEAR CREEK FISHERMAN
Michael's Collection

The Brown Bear Hunter

Walter Genlow was graduated from the university as an honor student after years of hard work. Now the diploma was his; it was framed and hanging on the wall as an important proof of his accomplishment.

It seems that luck followed him after the examinations, for he was offered a good job with an old manufacturing company, well known for the fine quality of its products. The superintendent of the company was an old-timer who had worked himself up from the ranks. He had not changed much in all those years—the same fellow, friendly and helpful.

Walter accepted the position. His job involved new methods of production which he started to work on immediately. After only two weeks' study, out came his ideas on a new manufacturing process. He stated, with vigor, that the old ways were too slow and too expensive. His sweeping program was immediately put into operation.

However, there was something wrong with his speed-up; and after the time-study had been checked, the shortcuts did not appear and the various manufactured parts did not carry the company's outstanding workmanship.

Well, that did not bother Walter too much. The time-study was off in the timing, of course, and the old fogeys running the machines were not on their toes. It certainly was a big drawback to have those old fellows in a plant! The worst part was that they did not have the proper respect for a highly educated man. If he gave strict orders to change the operation, they did not change it. They just did not pay attention to him. They went back to running the operation the old way.

Walter also noticed that when he came with his orders they did not show proper respect for him. Sometimes they just stood there smiling—no, it was not exactly a smile, more like a silly grin—as though they were saying, "Here comes our little boy again!" Well, those old fogeys certainly were not going to push him around! Nobody could do that!

A few days later he was in the superintendent's office with another new idea. In fact, it was already diagrammed on paper. Now, all he needed was the superintendent's approval, but somehow the latter was not greatly impressed and suggested that Walter talk it over with some of the fellows in the plant. For Walter, it was very insulting to suggest that he talk it over with the machine operators. What would they know about the process? The surprising fact was that the boss could have such a thought in mind, but then he didn't have any more education than the rest of them.

A week later, Walter was in the superintendent's office again, this time to suggest the older operators be replaced with younger men. He could not get anything done with such a gang! A smile glided over the superintendent's face. His gaze wandered out through the big window. The leaves on the maple tree outside were starting to dry and turn yellow, a sure sign of fall. After a time, he informed Walter that he could not fire those fellows and suggested that Walter talk to the foreman of the union. "Well," thought Walter, "this certainly is a new slant on things; if he were superintendent, those fellows would surely be out in a hurry!" There was one good attribute about Walter. If he decided to follow his convictions, there was no stopping him.

The meeting with the union foreman made Walter hopping mad. That jackass of a foreman had called him a young whippersnapper, and he'd told him that the sooner he picked up his marbles and got out of there, the better it would be for all concerned. That was the last straw! Of course, it was all clear to him now that the whole gang were Communists and of the worst kind.

That night he was walking the floor and pounding his fist on the table. The big question was, should he quit, just walk out, slam the door good and hard and tell them all to go to hell? But where would he go to get a well-paid job like this one? If only he could do something remarkable, something unusual, something that would make those men sit up and take notice. But what?

He happened to look through a sports magazine. There was a story about hunting the big bull moose. Well, to shoot a big moose was not his idea, but to be a great hunter was. He remembered the story of the past, when a big bear killed many farm animals, and a hunter tracked the bear down. He remembered the fascinating, thrilling story in which the bear attacked the hunter and ripped his coat to pieces. In the terrible scuffle, the hunter lost his gun and had only the hunting knife left. After an heroic struggle, he killed the beast with his knife and was hailed as a great hero. Everybody looked up to him. He had marks of the bear's claws and fangs all over his body.

Walter's mind was made up. He was going to kill a big bear. Then he would be a great hunter. Furthermore, the bear's head would be mounted and hung on the wall in his office, with grinning teeth and bare fangs showing. The sight certainly would scare the hell out of anybody, and, of course, everybody in the plant would have to see this great monster. He, of course, would be standing there smiling, and would be the toast of the whole factory, and his picture would be sprawling all over newspapers and magazines. His name would be repeated again and again over radio and television.

The next day he asked for one week off from his work, explaining that he was going bear hunting. The boss informed him that the plant could hardly run without him, but if it was important, he would have to let him go. He had to promise to be back in the plant one week from the day.

In the newspapers he saw that Duluth, Minnesota, was having trouble with bears, that they even roamed the streets. Now if he were there and a bear attacked some schoolchildren, he could kill the bear. Boy! What a story that would make! A long-distance telephone call to Duluth informed him that he could probably see some bears if he would drive out to the dump in the woods where the bears sometimes came for an evening meal.

Somehow this information dampened his notion of a great hunt. For him to go to a dump and shoot a bear—no, that was not his idea of a great bear hunt.

Nevertheless, the next morning a car roared through Minnesota. The driver had a firm grip on the steering wheel, his eyes glued to the road. He passed Minneapolis at a fast clip, heading north. In Fargo, he stopped for a bite to eat and mailed a card back to the plant stating that he had reached this city in record time. The following morning, halfway into Montana, he was informed that the bear country was farther northwest.

Twenty-four hours later, he and his guide were on the hunt, but there was no bear that day, not even tracks. The next day they saw a bear—frightened and running into a grove of trees. So the guide, after lots of screaming and banging on a tin can, scared the bear out. Walter missed the first shot, but two more brought him down. Walter stood there with his rifle ready. The guide walked over to the bear and proclaimed him dead. Now, all that was left was to skin the bear, cut the head off, and Walter could be on his way home.

The guide, who was a hunter of many years, advised Walter not to bother with the hide or the head, because it was all in a terrible mess and moreover, the unpleasantness would be enhanced because it was a warm day. Why not take pictures of it and let it go at that? Half a dozen pictures were taken showing Walter holding the bear's head in an upright position while holding the rifle in his other hand, so that there would be no doubt that he had indeed shot the bear.

He drove home in record time, stopping only for gasoline and a bite to eat. He could hardly wait to see the pictures developed. With some retouching they turned out fine and Walter lost no time in thumbtacking them all over the plant.

For Walter, it turned out to be a day he would never forget. Everyone in the plant laughed and made fun of the pictures. Some of the fellows even asked him where the mother of the cub was when he shot it.

This was it; he had had enough. Now he could understand the whole thing—why the guide did not want to skin the bear or cut off its head, and why those fellows in the plant laughed so long and loud. That night was a long one for Walter. By morning, he had made his decision. He must get away. He could not face anybody after what had happened. There was only one thing to do—clean out his office, get his check, and go.

When Walter came to the office and started to collect his things, his telephone was ringing. The superintendent would like to see him. So that was it! The superintendent was going to fire him! When Walter came into his office the big man was sitting at his desk. He greeted Walter and asked him to have a chair, as he looked him over very carefully. He noticed the pale face with the drawn lines in it. "Not much sleep for Walter," he thought. His friendly eyes had a faraway look in them as he gazed out the big window over the green field where a light-blue haze rose slowly in the morning sun. For some time he sat and said nothing.

Then he turned to Walter and asked him if he ever played football. When Walter said "no," he spoke of the eleven players on the team and the quarterback who called the signals. "A good quarterback must know what every member of the team can do and not do, so that he can call the right plays. We have the same need in the plant. We must know of each worker's ability to produce—his good points and his faults. It must be teamwork if we are to succeed. A quarterback can call the signals, but if he doesn't have somebody in the line to open up the holes for him, he doesn't get any place. In this plant we can give orders and in most cases the orders will be fulfilled. If we ask the different team members for co-operation, it will be teamwork that counts and it is what we are fortunate enough to have."

As far as the bear hunt is concerned, that is an old, old story. We have men in this country who spend thousands of dollars to get a record trophy. A trophy is a memorial of a contest, but there is no contest when on one side there is a fellow with all the newest inventions in hunting gear—airplanes, helicopters, field-glasses, high-powered rifles and ammunition, while on the other side there are no more defenses than there were a thousand years ago. The animals are so scared, so frightened for their lives they try to hide. There will be no change in this unfair, cowardly situation as long as men want to get their pictures in the papers, and as long as the newspapers and magazines glorify the trophy hunters.

As for destroying our natural resources, we are experts in that field and have been for years. When the lumber barons operated in this country, they cut down all the big trees and left nothing for windbreaks or reproduction. As a result, there are millions of acres of desolate brush country where no timber grows, where in the olden days the immense trees were standing tall and thick.

The same thing is happening today in regard to our wild game. The trophy hunters are ruthlessly killing off all the biggest specimens and soon only the small and the dwarfed will be left. If the farmers in America had started some years ago to kill off all of the biggest and best farm animals, or shipped them to slaughterhouses, what would we have in this country today? Where would be the enormous big bulls, the blue ribbon cows, the famous stallions, the outstanding rams and boars?

In this work to save our magnificent wild creatures, we need teamwork and cooperation from all. We must imprint on peoples' minds that the great trophy hunter is a misinformed human being. Right now we are hundreds of years behind. When the majority of citizens understand that one of those big, beautiful wild animals alive is worth ten thousand heads hanging on a wall, then and then only, will the wilderness produce its lovely and fascinating life.

Many snows have melted in the woods since that day in the office when Walter brought down on his own head roars of derision. The superintendent has passed on, but his spirit remains, and there is the same old teamwork, the consideration for all in the now huge, sprawling plant. A new man is the boss. His name is Walter Genlow. On the wall in his elegant office hangs a picture that really doesn't belong there. It is the picture of a young man holding up a dead bear in a sitting position.

The other day when Walter's wife asked why he had that homely picture hanging in his office, his answer was, "It is to remind me of what was once the size of my hat. It is my anchor and the guide in my life's progress."

"ALONG THE CREEK" — Collection of Midwest Lumber Company

Can the Nine Mile Creek Be Saved?

Like a great artery, the Nine Mile Creek winds its way through the city of Bloomington, through woods, fields and forest—through swamps and marshes, creating small water pools and lakes that blink like mirrors in the sun. Sometimes the creek is in a hurry, dives over small rapids, over stones and sandbars, then through the lowlands. It wanders with all the time in the world—slowly winding its way—not in a hurry any more. When it dives into the river, it is no more.

I still remember forty years ago on a hot and humid July day when I first came to know the wonderful Nine Mile Creek. To me it was like a small river, with great determination, bubbling and gushing around through the deep forest on its way to the river bottom.

The water it offered was cold, clear and pure—a constant flow of precious drink, not only for the thirsty landscape but also for cattle, wild animals and birds. In its wandering it created many of the old swimming holes, where the young boys were diving, swimming and wading. There was no restriction on swimming suits or short jeans in those days—it was a free country. Why bother with those things? A carefree world for a young generation!

The fishing was good . . . not any fancy fishing poles—just a long stick with a line and a worm on the hook. In the spring when the trout were running, then fishermen, young and old, standing on bridges and the shore, all had a good time.

The Beaver Brook Addition, where the arm from the northeast meets the flow from the west, some years ago contained a small waterfall about four to five feet high. Many times in the early morning I have stood and listened to those wonderful sounds of the gushing rumble from the waterfall—a grand solo in nature's manifold sounds. Sometimes in early spring it sounded like the waterfall was mumbling . . . laughing . . . giggling under the snow cover, happy because the spring was coming.

To the west of Normandale in the marshes, years ago, was a nice shimmering blue lake—a creation of a beaver colony—with a dam, a hut, an interesting project, a study of nature in conservation. People from many states and foreign countries gazed on this wonderful project . . . unbelievable they would say—a wilderness in the middle of a bustling city.

Now the beaver colony and the dam are no more. Dry and desolate lies the lake bed with old tree stumps and watersoaked sticks on the bottom. Often ducks and geese circle the old homestead looking for the small, blue lake where they used to build their nests and raise their young. They don't know that on an Easter morning three adventuresome high school boys in their rubber raft conquered the interesting project and with their ax and other tools destroyed the dam and the beaver hut and slaughtered the beavers. If the boys sold the furs, they would get a few dollars — money bearing the inscription, "In God We Trust."

The Nine Mile watershed was rich with wild animals and birds . . . rich with swamps, marshes and a chain of small lakes, one after the other like pearls on a string. The waterflow was very constant. Even in dry summers the creek was impressive. Too bad it could not last—but the big building boom came sweeping over the land. Like a gigantic bulldozer it leveled everything in its path—hills, knolls—filling in ravines, marshes and lakes. All the natural beauty of the landscape disappeared. The green, lustrous forest where the trees were standing thick and tall were leveled off. Often not a single tree was left standing. Roads, streets and avenues had to be built. The few lakes that were left, as a rule, were isolated . . . landlocked. The bulldozers, turnapulls and the draglines were the rulers of the land. The beautiful Nine Mile Creek was fast facing destruction and would soon vanish into oblivion.

Then it happened that the gallant staff from the *Bloomington Sun* started a campaign to save the precious brook from total destruction. Through their great efforts the citizens of Bloomington, Edina, Eden Prairie, Hopkins and Minnetonka were aroused and they demanded that something be done. Committees were appointed and soon the Nine Mile Creek Watershed manager was in the driver's seat. It looked successful for a time, although great obstacles had to be overcome.

Many snows have melted since that time . . . the brook does not laugh and giggle any more. Small and deceived, it is rolling slow and shamefaced through the landscape, soon to be forgotten.

A new and very clever slogan appeared on the horizon—"You Cannot Stop Progress." A new weapon and a new onslaught of our natural resources, a smart way to brainwash people. Today the eager beavers are at it again, chopping away, digging, scooping up, filling in the swamps and marshes. All along the creek men and machines are at work.

Also another very clever way has been found to replace the marshes and the swamps—replace them with a small shallow lake — the so-called mudflats. The marshes, swamps and the natural lakes cannot be replaced except by great water reservoirs which control the outflow. The marshes collect moisture. In rain and snow, in storms, they work like a great sponge collecting and storing tremendous quantities of water. Then in a dry season they filter and then let the water slowly out— cold and clear. Now it is a different story with all the diking and filling in, the water in the creek is now brown in color and dirty. We should have learned from the sad saga of so many Minnesota creeks that have vanished, and taken precautions.

Some time in the future the Nine Mile Creek will disappear. The creek bed will be a storm sewer where the water in heavy rains and spring floods will rush and roar on to the river bottom. In the dry seasons there will be many small pools of dirty, stinky water standing in the slimy creek bed.

With sadness, so many of our citizens will remember this historic landmark as it was in the yesteryears—a precious jewel in a gorgeous landscape. Again the young generation has drawn the short straw for preservation of their American heritage—it seems that they are always the losers.

No, the beautiful creek did not die, but it had to get worse before it could be improved. It so happened that a tank truck with 2400 gallons of acid burst open and the poison was dumped into the creek. That ought to be the act of the mercy-killing of a dying stream.

But not so. The Bloomington Natural Resources Commission heard the cry from the mutilated creek and called for action. A special meeting was summoned and the angry members demanded that something be done and as soon as possible. Of course, for many people interested in conservation it seemed a hopeless case. The Nine Mile Creek Watershed managers had tried for many years to take care of the creek, but with very little success. The laws and rules to protect our lakes and streams are very weak and they had only a limited power and authority to do what should be done.

It was decided that the interested people for the preservation of the creek must be aroused and of course the *Bloomington Sun,* now as before, took up the battle cry with Frances Berns in the front line. A meeting was called in the Bloomington Council Chambers and the Nine Mile Creek Citizens' Committee was formed with delegates from Edina, Eden Prairie, Hopkins, Minnetonka and Bloomington. Mrs. Shirley Hunt was elected foreman, Olav Wallo, vice-foreman, and Frances Blacklock, secretary.

It was the start on a long and cumbersome road with many failures, setbacks and despair. But it was a determined bunch of fighters. They had decided to do something to save the stream. Then came the month of August. There was a lot of rain and flooding. The marshes, swamps and lakes were filled to overflowing and the creek really came to life again. It was a wonderful sight and sound as the water bubbled and gushed over stones, boulders and sandbars. It was just like the olden days. And that is the way it should be.

But the rejoicing came to an abrupt end because all along the stream arose an unbearable stench, a terrible odor so that people all along the stream had to close their doors and windows and move inside. No more picnicking along the creek or no more wading or playing in the water for the youngsters. Maybe the very worst part was the sight of hundreds of fish, dead or dying in the stream. Some of the poor creatures had leaped from the horrible water with its stench and were now taking their last breath, dying on the shoreline. There certainly was a bewildered bunch of people who lived along the creek that day. All were wondering, with a kind of horror, about the stench.

The Bloomington Health Department had tested the water and informed the

Natural Resources Commission that the polluted material was human waste. This certainly was shocking news and there was some doubt about the test because they were wondering how anybody could be so dirty as to dump all the raw sewage into the stream. The mystery seemed to increase because in a few days the odor disappeared as fast as it had appeared. By this time the people interested in the creek were really furious about the whole puzzle.

Then it happened. The bomb exploded. The Citizens' Committee had a meeting and at that meeting they were informed that one of the communities had had some trouble with their overflowing sewer and the only relief was to open the valve and dump the raw sewage into the stream. Now all our citizens really got the full impact of what we were doing to our environment.

With a strong backing from the interested people, the Nine Mile Creek District managers took action and demanded that the Minnesota Pollution Control Agency do something about it and they called two hearings in connection with the pollution. And the friends of the creek came with a strong demand that the filth dumped into the stream must be stopped.

So it happened that after the second hearing, the County Attorney informed the guilty party that it must remove the pipe and valve connection to the creek. Not only that, but all those factories along the stream received strict orders: "No more dumping of polluted material into the creek!"

Then came the beautiful May day we all had been looking forward to. The Edina Park and Recreation Committee had tested the water and found it clean enough to stock the stream with 300 trout. The Nine Mile Creek Citizens' Committee had taken a long step in the right direction. But we now have a long and cumbersome road ahead of us, but we also know the Nine Mile Creek Citizens Committee never gives up.

On an early morning, I wandered along the creek. The haze was rising slowly from the lowlands. Dewdrops, like pearls, clung to the green blades and I was looking and listening to the stream. It had changed its tune—not the sorrowful sob and the lonely cry any more. A little subdued it was, but with some glad laughter and giggling. Happy it was, because it had found some friends that really cared.

The Nuisance Hunter and Trapper

For the experienced hunter with many years in the field and forest, the nuisance hunter is a tag-along, a person who should never carry a gun or fire a shot. As a rule he has no experience in the woods, has seldom fired a gun and has very little knowledge of wildlife. On a hunting expedition he soon gets tired of looking, tired of being quiet and tired of not seeing or hearing anything. So the first chance he gets he fires the gun at anything that walks or flies: "Fire first and then look!" For him, if he shoots a man or cripples an animal, it is all in the day's work. His attitude is: "So what?" It is because of this irresponsible hunter's gun that there are numerous deer rotting in the woods and fields. As an example of this irresponsibility, some years ago, on a cold winter day, a beautiful young dog was brought to the veterinarian after being gone for three days. His front paw had been securely locked in a new steel trap for seventy-two hours. The temperature ranged from fourteen to twenty below zero. Of course, for the nuisance hunter who had set the trap, it was too cold to go back and check. He was sitting in a nice home and sleeping in a warm bed. He did not have to worry.

When he finally found the dog in the trap, he thought it was a wild animal and fired an arrow. The arrow lodged in the dog's shoulder blades but it did not kill him. The dog was freed by somebody and at last found his way home, the sharp blade of the arrow still lodged in his shoulder blade. After this ordeal, the dog never recovered and was put to sleep. It was discovered later that this terrible hunter's gear was a Christmas present to the young boy from his father. Those ghastly traps most certainly must have looked wonderful under the tree with the greetings, "Peace on Earth" ringing out—but only for human beings. For the wild animals it meant suffering, pain and death.

A couple of years ago two boys set six of their Christmas gift traps in the woods around a fox den near my home. I live in a game refuge and, of course, I sprung the traps as soon as the boys were out of the woods. It was a winter of deep snow and it took the boys seven days to return to their traps. If a wild animal had been caught, it would have been in the trap for a whole week.

Those traps are still there, fastened to some wooden poles with strong steel wires. But they are harmless now, smashed to pieces by a twelve-pound sledge hammer. If one condemned the boys, he would be wrong. A child's heart, mind and soul are like deep, rich black soil after a warm rain. The fertile soil is waiting for the sun, the good seed that will soon sprout, the flowers that will bloom and the trees that will grow. This is the time for wildlife education to begin, in the homes and in the schools.

Conservation

He was very old and walked with short, cautious steps. His face was wrinkled from many, many years and a long span of life. His long hair and whiskers were silver-gray in color and tousled. His thoughtful gaze under bushy eyebrows had seen all and forgotten nothing, remembering things often so clearly, like pearls on a string. He has seen great nations born, then tumbled and dispersed, and generations have followed generations in a span of countless centuries. His name is Father Time.

He is leading a very young man by the hand whose name is New Year. They are on their way to a mountaintop where Father Time will show the youngster many lands and oceans and inform him about the different nations, folkways and treasure.

He is pointing to a big country, large but not rich. The ruler of that country is Mr. Foolish. He has four sons, whose names are: Wasteful, Careless, Selfish, and Greedy. Of natural resources there is very little saved. Often they have had to scrape the bottom of the barrel for crumbs that were left from the destructive days. Through the years they have wasted the country's resources, as though there were no end, as though tomorrow would never come, or the next generation would never be born.

Father Time is pointing to another country. The manager is Mr. Wisdom who has three sons: Sensible, Careful, and Forward-Looking. The land is still rich in natural resources. Of coal and iron and mining products, there is enough to last for many generations. The swamps and lowlands are never touched; there is no dragging or digging of channels. They filter and hold back the water, controlling the flow of clean, cold pure water wandering its way through mountains, woods and fields, through towns and villages. It forms shimmering blue lakes, offering precious drink to a healthy nation, and moisture to the landscape.

The enormous woods are deep green and lustrous with trees standing thick and tall. They have used common sense—the sensible cutting method and left large trees standing for seeding and windbreaks. Where a tree is cut, a seedling is planted. On the farms the soil is deep and rich, producing big crops. There are no gullies, no run-off of topsoil. No dust storms or dust bowls in that country. Some sad experiences have been their teacher and they have also listened to time-tested advice. Now they know how.

The woods, fields and mountains are rich in wild game. The lakes and streams are well stocked with fish. And behind the project to preserve the wildlife, there have been not only single persons, clubs and societies, but the whole country. The youngsters of this country have had imprinted in their minds the necessity to guard their wonderful heritage, the wild animals, fish and birds. That is a very important subject in education from the grade schools through high schools and universities.

They harvest their wildlife with careful planning and control from year to year, a system whereby both the quantity and quality have been very constant. In that program, they have moved and replanted thousands of small or large animals from one territory to another, where the different species have a better chance to live and reproduce. And not so long ago, the leaders of that country have declared war on air and water pollution with a tough and hard program. They claim that within three years they will have eliminated pollution in lakes and streams and from the air, with stinky fumes and smog, so that the citizens of that country can again breathe healthy fresh air and drink clean water. The land's natural beauty is jealously guarded by all the citizens. It is the nation's pride fiercely defending a beloved heritage.

The old man and the young man have been on top of the mountain for a long time.

Now New Year wanted to know the name of this wonderful country that Father Time has shown him. Father Time looked at him with a happy gleam in his eyes and said: "That country's name, my boy, let us call it Conservation's Land."

The Virgin Wilderness

In many states, far-sighted people have for years tried to secure certain territory, a field or forest or mountain, where the wilderness still whispers, where primeval ages exist unchanged by civilization's destructive and greedy powers. It certainly is a tragedy that so little is left of this country's great natural resources. Sometime in the future when the younger generation awakens to the full impact of what has happened to their land, their inheritance, they will point a finger and demand to know what we have done with the millions of acres of forest that the lumber barons ravaged and laid waste. They will ask about the rich iron mines that were so terribly exploited, now a thing of the past. They will ask about the clean, beautiful lakes that disappeared, big and small.

Yes, even the great rivers are little more than sewers after they pass through our cities. And what was once a blue, shimmering lake downstream is now nothing more than a great, slimy cesspool where fish die by the thousands. They will ask what happened to the rich black soil that some years ago covered our farmland. They will also inquire about our disappearing wildlife. They will want to know what happened to those billions of wild creatures, the big game that used to roam the plains, or the small ones that were so happy in the forest not so very long ago.

They will point their fingers at you: "What is your answer? What excuse do you have? You were the guardian of our inheritance, the custodian of this great and wonderful land so rich in natural resources!"

It is difficult to belive that so young a country, so rich in resources, is now almost reduced to a state in which the bottom of the barrel must be scraped for crumbs that are left from earlier devastation.

There are some far-sighted people in this country who are willing to preserve the land's resources. They plead and ask and beg to save some for the coming generation. These gallant people with hearts of gold are fighting against overwhelming odds —fighting big business, the great electrical utility companies, the lumber and mining interests and the lobbyists. Big money talks and talks big. These champions, the trailblazers for conservation and for wilderness preservation never give up. They have formed clubs and started organizations, holding meetings and discussions. If it were not for these gallant fighters, our great country would have no wilderness today.

In the meantime, the greedy horde of despoilers are smiling in satisfaction over all this time-wasting talk, with no anxiety. The lumber baron is not dead. The whine of the chain saws in the wilderness is still heard and thousands of our great timbers are crashing to earth. Slowly but surely, they are chopped away. Roads must be built to haul out the lumber. Logging roads, like a big snake, twist and turn into the heart of the wilderness. Soon jeeps and automobiles are crawling in, exploring new territories. With the automobile comes the litterbugs, the firebugs and the trigger-happy with guns and ammunition. The bulldozers will be crawling in and the wide road will be ready. The blue, crystal-clear lake is converted into a racetrack for the speedboats where the roar from the motors and the screams and hollering of the waterskiers can be heard for miles. The shoreline will soon be lined with tin cans, paper trash and garbage. Civilization is on the move!

Maybe it would be of interest to find out what other countries are doing with their wilderness and how they defend and protect their inheritance. There is one thing certain—when it comes to protecting their wilderness, they do not give an inch. Eastern Normarka, the waste wilderness just outside Oslo, Norway, with its streams, lakes, woods and timberland, has no inside roads, only hiking trails in all directions. And, of course, on the trails, they do not allow signs to spoil the scenery, only colored markings on trees and boulders. In summer or winter you will find thousands of hikers on the trail, carrying their food and other equipment on their backs, a healthy and strong people, on the march!

Some years ago a big electric company asked permission from the Norwegian government to cut a swath sixty feet wide in the forest for their electric line to be erected through eastern Normarka. The wilderness defenders there did not waste any time talking or holding meetings. They staged a torchlight parade, sixty thousand strong, through Oslo and demanded that the Government put an immediate stop to the electric company's project. I am sure you can guess what happened. Today, the electric line skirts outside Normarka, even though the distance is miles longer.

We need the Quetico-Superior Canoe Wilderness badly. We need it as it has been for years, a wilderness for canoe travelers and hikers, a paradise. There is no middle of the road here. If motor, speed and pontoon boats and snowmobiles are permitted, within five short years the wilderness will be gone.

To ask the canoe, the sailboat and rowboats to share our lakes with motor-driven craft would be like asking the thousands of bicyclists to share our superhighways with the automobile. In short, the wilderness friends and the outdoors-loving people would disappear in no time. We must not harbor the faulty conclusion that the motoring public would pilot their craft with courtesy and consideration for all. The golden rule of gentlemanly behavior is lost and forgotten on our lake shores.

If we study sports competitions in the United States, we realize that the average youth does not belong on the football, basketball, hockey or baseball teams, for with few exceptions, these are very big, tall and heavy fellows. In general, today sports have very little room for the small or average-sized young person, except as spectators.

Anyone who has love and admiration for a healthy and strong America should spend a few days on the canoe routes and watch the crews paddle their long, smooth craft with fast strokes over the blue shimmering lakes, heading for those unknown regions. Young and old, strong and healthy, sunburned and smiling — here size and weight are not the deciding factors. Only the wilderness is calling. And a long hike on a peaceful trail into the primitive forest is a challenge and a bright adventure to everybody. They love and respect the wilderness and all it stands for. Such an outing is a never-to-be-forgotten experience.

Would it be too much to ask, in a humble way, that the few million acres of wilderness be left as it has been for thousands of years? After all, it is only a small part, a small piece of an enormous country. Maybe someday Young America will stand on a high hill or a small mountaintop and look out over the quiet and peaceful wilderness, a breathtaking panorama in all its splendor. And here for the first time in history, the custodians of this great country would not have to bow their heads in shame, but could proclaim that we have saved something for future generations.

RUFFED GROUSE AT SUNDOWN
D. H. M. Eames Collection

The Sports Hunter

Somebody has said: "The hunter shoots in sport but the animal dies in earnest."

The small boat slides smooth and feather-like over Hide-Away Lake in the wilderness. In the rear of the boat, sitting rather low, with a pillow behind his back, is the skipper, and in the bottom of the boat are a couple of beer cans in a cooler and a lunch bucket. A bashful breeze ripples over the crystal-clear water. The red sail fulls out at the mast. Small waves lap like wet tongues against the boat's side.

It is so quiet, so peaceful on the warm October day—only the skipper, the blue lake and the small white clouds drifting leisurely over the wide horizon.

For John this is the life worth living. For more than three hundred days in the year he is the vice-president of a big company. It is a tough job, highly competitive, and nerve-wracking. But today all is forgotten. His office with all its trouble is so far from his mind. John is in another world, sailing free as a bird on outstretched wings. He sees the virgin forest, deep green and lustrous, the beautiful hills and small mountains. Creeks and rivers are there, tumbling out into the deep lake and disappearing. He sees it all unfolding like a film on a screen. This is his first sailing this year— a long dream finally come true. It is his eighth year on Hide-Away Lake in the hunting season.

He and six other fellows formed a hunting club. They have a beauty of a hunting cabin built between a point on the lake and a small river, with its waterfall bubbling out on the west side of the cabin. They own the lake and all of the surrounding territory. The road into the lake is long and narrow, hard to find and moss-grown. It is nine years since John and Arthur started the club, which is for sports hunters only. In the cabin there is no telephone, radio or television; and no visitors or guests are welcome. The rules and regulations of the club are quite simple: (1) One must be a devoted friend of the wilderness, and (2) One must act and behave like a gentleman. The members are selected and screened with utmost care. There are seven members. That is the limit. No more. There is a long waiting list of those who would like to belong. Some of the members are married, in which case they spend their summer vacations with their families—that is an unwritten law. However, in the hunting season they are free. That is the reason the Hide-Away Lake Hunting Club has been a huge success.

Ed, who writes for a big newspaper, is often referred to as the Father of Outdoor Writers in the Great Northwest. A rugged individual, carved right out of the wilderness itself, he has for years been a trailblazer for the preservation of wildlife and a stout defender of the unknown region. He has started many worthwhile outdoor organizations; and besides, through his writing he tells the saga of the wilderness which he knows so well.

Cap, who is a man with vast knowledge and understanding of the wilderness, has traveled in many states and foreign countries. He has hiked the lonely trail and has paddled his big canoe over the long and seemingly endless lakes and rivers. Always on the go to arouse interest in wilderness problems, he is helpful to his fellow men and is a true ambassador of the Great Outdoor Wonderland.

Willis is an eminent symphony conductor and one of the finest violin artists in America. He has long tried to grasp and capture in composition the wilderness' manifold sounds. He has listened to a bubbling brook in spring, mumbling under the snow-cover, and in the bright moonlight, to the bashful waves in their mushing squirts rolling upon the sandy shores. He has listened to the breeze from the open sea on a warm, sunny summer day. But most of all, he has listened to the wilderness' silent language — maybe a sorrowful tone — toward the end of the fleeing summer.

Roger is a nationally famous painter. He has captured the Hide-Away Lake landscape on his canvas, and these paintings are often a collector's item. Every Christmas one of the club members receives one of these beautiful paintings, mysterious, soft, bejeweled. It is like a fresh breath of air from the Northland.

Roy is a contractor and architect. He designed and built the Hide-Away Lake cabin. He is the businessman of the club, and a good one, an easy-going fellow, likeable and always in good humor. His hobby at Hide-Away Lake for the last five years has been to build an old-time flour mill, complete with waterwheel, grinding stones, hoppers and chutes, a perfect example of a real old-timer.

From the cabin on the lake to the waterfall where he built the mill is a good mile, so most of the material has been hauled in during the winter. The mill is built of logs, selected and hauled from the forest. Roy has visited many lands and countries. His idea for this flour mill came from a small community in Finland where he was on tour in connection with one of his projects. It was winter in Finland and the bus in which Roy was riding was snowbound in a small village. The hotel was closed for the winter, but the goodhearted Finns welcomed Roy into their homes. It took many days before the road was cleared and the bus could be on its way again. Meanwhile, they had a wonderful time. He admired these hardy, healthy people, so full of energy, young and old on skis and skates. They never figure distance in miles—but in time. It so happened that he had his slides from America with him—towns and country, big factories, farms and prairies, universities and schools, field and stream. A big hall was provided for Roy to show his films and slides. People came from long distances to view the United States of America, for they had never seen it. The food they served was very good and the bread and pancakes were particularly delicious. Of course, Roy had to find out what the bread was made of and in this way he stumbled on to this old grinding mill where nothing was taken out or added to the flour. On the farms where they raised the grain —rye, barley, oats and peas—no chemical fertilizers were ever used, only the natural environment, and of course, there was no spreading of poison from weed killers. The grain was unspoiled from Mother Nature's gifts of life and health.

Roy took some pictures of the mill and made some sketches — from the inside. It was an interesting experience for him. The day he left the village, many new-found friends for both America and Roy were there to say good-bye, and many of them brought small gifts—memories of Finland, a land of proud and hardy people, memories from the blue shimmering lakes and the endless forests. He also had a recipe for the wonderful tasting bread and the pancakes.

The next fall, Roy received a small sack of flour from his friends in Finland, a gift to him and to his friends at Hide-Away Lake. The gift came as a surprise, and after the bread was baked and everyone had had a slice or two, they all agreed it certainly tasted good. That evening a long and interesting discussion took place about the flour and the bread. All were in agreement on one point—that in flour and bread often too much of the health-giving life was processed out and removed. They also wondered what effect all the chemical fertilizers and the spreading of poison crops would do to the human race.

Roy suggested that the Hide-Away Lake Club buy a farm and raise its own crops with no poison or chemical fertilizers to be used. He himself promised to build a flour mill—a real old-time type—grinding stones and all. This project, which had been in operation for three years, certainly has been a great success. The 100-acre farm is deep in the woods, not far away from Hide-Away Lake. The house, which is modern, is built of timber and the barn is painted red, both new. In the corral are some strong, fast-footed horses, chestnut in color, and in the pasture some select cattle graze. No, there is no tractor on this farm.

We must not forget a very important man whose name is Joe. He is a free-born son of the wilderness itself, a full-blooded Indian, born and reared in this part of the country, an outstanding hunter, fisherman and handyman. He is just like one of the members. Every Christmas, a whole truck-load of presents arrives for him and his family. Of course, he is always looking forward to the two weeks in town, for right after Christmas he celebrates the holidays with visits to the city homes of the club members.

Arthur is a famous radio and television star. Every morning at about nine or ten o'clock, he wanders in the woods to a certain place where there is an old deer-trail that has been traveled for many years. In an opening in the woods, a few yards from the beaten path, stands a tree stump, just the right height for a good seat. Here is Arthur's outpost, the most dangerous place in the woods for deer. When he has lighted his pipe and had a nice long talk with the chickadees and his other feathered friends, a magnificent buck comes tiptoeing into view. He stands there looking at the hunter for some time. Art notices that he has improved from last year. He has one more prong on his antlers, six points now.

Art just loves the beautiful creature—the marvelous head with its lofty crown, a picture of grace and elegance. This is Art's friend. He comes every year to welcome Art to Hide-Away Lake. After some time, he tells the buck to move on—"Come again tomorrow"—and like a ballet dancer, the deer is soon out of sight. This is Art's temple. He knows and understands the wilderness and the fauna. To fire a shot here would be to offend the God-given peacefulness. That sacred landscape! Everything here is as dear to him as his oldest friends. He has come here every year for eight years.

John and his sailboat resemble a taxicab in town. They are always on the go. In the morning he pilots Ed over the lake to the mountains where Ed steps ashore and gathers enough firewood for his coffee on his way up to the top. From the mountains he can see for miles and miles in all directions—over endless forests and many lakes, streams, and far out on the horizon where there is a blue lake, enormously big. This is Ed's kingdom. From this mountaintop, his best editorials are written. Here he can sit day after day happily and dreamily writing, never tiring of all this beauty. Here his hungry soul can find a permanent anchoring place.

From John's sailboat, Roger the painter, has found many excellent motifs for his paintings. It might be a waterfall thundering into the lake or some shoreline where the majestic Norway pines lift their crowns to the highest azure heaven. It could be a black bear on the shoreline, standing and taking scent, with some bear cubs playing, rolling and wrestling in the clearing. Or it could be an enormous moose in a lily pond, munching some water lilies, standing with his head raised high, the mighty shovel-rack painted against the blue horizon like a great mogul, a supreme ruler looking over his empire.

The evening is almost the best time of the day for the members. After an excellent dinner, they gather around a good fire outside the cabin with their pipes and cigars and listen to each other's contributions of song, music and stories. This is a group of men rich in talent, high culture and grand fellowship. For three weeks they live in their own exclusive world where the best of brotherly feeling is brought forth.

Only when the last evening at Hide-Away Lake approaches, does a somewhat dampened feeling settle over the gathering. It will be a long, long time until the next hunting trip next fall. The following morning when they are ready to leave, Joe is packing some deer meat in their cars. It might be appreciated if a member invites some guest for a venison dinner. After all, it is a hunting club. John is the last to leave the camp. It is a sad, sad day for him, and he takes a long time to do his packing. The mast on his sailboat has to be taken down, the sail put away, the boat sandpapered and dragged into the cabin. It will be painted fresh next summer, but that time seems far away. He starts the car, drives slowly over the narrow bridge crossing the river. When he reaches the bend in the road, he stops the car and steps out for the last look. It is as though he would see and remember everything and keep it alive forever in his mind just as it is. He sees the log cabin standing there, so big and sturdy, so inviting with the setting sun reflecting a warm glow on the closed windows.

The deep blue lake is so still and peaceful, framed in a rich splendor of colors from the autumn's generous display. The hills and mountains seem so trustworthy, so majestic in proud repose, awaiting the winter's white satin robe. From the west, over the big lake, comes the evening breeze, gently rustling through the forest, tiptoes between branches, whispers the autumn's sad and lonely tune. Still and soft, the yellow, red and golden leaves flutter down, settle on the river, sailing like tiny ships on to the peaceful fjord.

He also listens to the wilderness' soft and gentle ways; it whispers now as though to ask: "Do you leave us now? Do you prefer the swarm, the crowd, the city's grime and noise to this?"

With a deep sigh, John whispers: "I will come back. I must come back."

The Bow-and-Arrow Hunter

There is a fairly new fad and another hunting tribe swarming over the horizon that is unknown in other civilized countries. These are the thrill seekers, the publicity hounds, men and women of all ages, shapes and sizes, pretending to be the great Robin Hood or William Tell.

Some of them, of course, are not satisfied with a friendly competition on the archery range. No, they must have a live target! It is such a thrill and "so fascinating" to have a chance to ram a horrible arrow into an innocent creature or bird. No other civilized country would permit the hunting of its wildlife with a bow and arrow. Such cruelly flimsy hunting gear is a reproduction of a model from the dark ages. In many lands and in some hunting clubs and wildlife organizations, they have displayed the famous picture: "Today's Buffalo Hunting With Bow and Arrow in the U.S.A." It demonstrates, with severity, our absolute disregard for our wildlife and the humane treatment of animals. It seems impossible to those people in kinder countries that some supposedly civilized people could stage a gruesome spectacle in which a young buffalo has to run between the hunters that are lined up to take a shot at the flying animal and at last when the buffalo reaches the end of the line, a hunter with a high-powered rifle kills him. But not before 52 arrows are sticking out all over the poor animal!

Many European countries have each year passed stricter laws about hunting methods and equipment, and have rigid tests for marksmanship. Furthermore, the hunters must have a thorough knowledge of wildlife and of the wilderness itself.

Today we have rifles and guns to harvest our wild game. While these weapons for hunting are not perfect, they are the best available. They have been tested and improved from year to year and also their ammunition. But the bow and arrow hunting gear has remained basically the same during the last thousand years. The longbow, as it was called, was never meant to be a dependable, accurate weapon for hunting. Its easy reloading and firing has made it popular. No person would rightfully compare the rifle and the bow as to accuracy. There are men who can step off fifty steps and hit a bull's-eye with an arrow, providing there is no wind and the target is over level ground, but such men are few and far between.

If people could witness the deer hunting horde that streams out in the field and forest when the bow-and-arrow season starts, it would be a terrifying sight. So many are amateur, inexperienced, would-be hunters! There is no control, no qualifying test. Anybody with enough money to purchase a bow and arrow and a license, is permitted to try his luck on any animal, big or small. For these hunters, the main thing is to hit the animal any place—in front, broadside or behind.

After the bow-and-arrow season, there are scores of deer, dead or dying in our woods. Some are crippled and limping around waiting for death; some are mercifully killed by the regular deer hunters; others are hidden and never discovered. In many meat lockers in this country, there is a gruesome collection of arrowheads found in deer carcasses. Some are new and shiny. The old and rusty ones have been lodged in the animals for years.

In the fall when the bow-and-arrow season starts, as a rule, there is no snow and no way for the hunter to track down the wounded animal, especially without a good tracking dog—but the use of a dog is against the law. It is not necessary to go back a thousand years in our progress just to satisfy those thrill seekers. Let us make it clear here and now that to hunt, to kill or wound a deer is not the same thrill as to play a slot machine and wait for the jackpot. I cannot see that it is a pleasure to plunge a horrible-looking arrowhead into a beautiful animal. To do so shows with glaring clarity a careless disregard for our wild animals.

The important thing for a good hunter (with a rifle) is to make a clean shot. One must know his own ability as a marksman, the distance or range, the specifications of hunting gear and ammunition, the wind's direction and where to aim the shot for instant death. If one can say after the shot, "The animal never knew what hit him"—that is the main thing. That is the way it should be. No wounding, no suffering, no crippling!

Why not compare our hunting laws for the protection of wildlife with those of some of the foremost countries of the world? In general, the European rules are as follows:

1. For hunting deer or bigger animals, the rifle bore must be at least 6½ mm. with special ammunition.

2. No person under fifteen years of age is permitted in the field and the forest dur-

ing hunting season, not even when accompanied by seasoned hunters.

3. Boys from fifteen to eighteen years of age are permitted in the forest and field during the hunting season, if accompanied by seasoned hunters, but they must not carry a gun or fire a shot.

4. Boys over eighteen years of age can hunt if they have the approval of the hunting supervisors' board, but they must have a certificate for marksmanship and the safe handling of a gun. The rifle must be of the right bore (not undersized) and also have the recommended ammunition. The hunter must have a thorough knowledge of the field and forest and be familiar with the wildlife.

5. Every hunting party must have a good tracking dog in case the deer or moose is wounded and on the run. The hunter must wait at least two hours before he takes the dog and starts tracking the animal down. As a rule, if a deer or bigger animal is wounded, it will run only a short distance and then lie down. After two hours it is often so stiff it is hard to get up and start running again.

6. No hunter must leave a wounded animal that has disappeared. It must be tracked down and put out of its misery before the hunter can start to look for new game.

That is the law of many lands—the foremost ones—when it comes to humane treatment of our wild game.

Many years must come and go before the U.S.A. will have laws like these, and by that time there will be no wild game left.

With the permission of the late Robert Murphy, reporter for the *Minneapolis Star*, we pass along his comments concerning Germany's strict hunting laws, rules and regulations:

Ramstein, Germany: "Nature is fascinating in a land where things are different but in general similar to our own area. This region, for instance, is mantled with evergreens, walking up the hills and covering the valleys. They are jealously guarded. Anyone caught poaching one is in for a good bit of trouble. They're harvested, though, according to a century's-old program and you'll find the logs stripped and de-barked, lying in roadside areas where they may rest for a couple of years to cure . . .

"Each district has a 'forstmeister,' head forester, who decides what trees shall be harvested and who has a lot of other duties. He superintends planting and you'll see a lot of fields of young trees awaiting replanting. The forstmeister is also the boss in hunting matters and the procedure here would drive some of my ardent deer-hunting friends wild. There are two types of deer, the hirsch, a large one similar to an elk, and the reh, a miniature animal which may dress out at only 20 or 30 pounds. The population of them is carefully controlled. Frequently along German roads you'll see a triangular sign in red warning you that wild animals may be found on the highway. There's no lettering, simply the silhouette of a leaping, antlered deer. The sign indicating that domestic animals may be at large has the silhouette of a cow . . .

"'To hunt the deer you must attend a 'jaegerschule,' hunter's school, with a minimum of twenty hours of classwork, after which you take a stiff examination. Then you may qualify for a permit that will cost you around $50. That isn't all it will cost you. Having obtained a permit, you check with the game office and are told where you may hunt— an area that forstmeisters' reports show has an excess population of animals. It may be two or three hundred miles away. Once there you don't just go into the woods and bang away. The forstmeister goes with you, and he points out the animal that you may shoot, often one not in its prime and just as well out of the herd. If you shoot it, there's a brief reverent ceremony, dating to mythological times, that winds up with a sprig of evergreen put in the animal's mouth. But that's not your deer. It still belongs to the state and for your pains you get only the trophy, the head. If you want the venison, you may pay for it at the going rate. Most restaurants have hirsch or reh dishes available because a deer was sold by the forstmeister on the open market."

PHEASANTS IN AN AUTUMN MARSH

Collection of Wildlife of America

Pheasants and the Old Gun

Silent, neglected and forsaken hangs the old gun on the wall. That is the way it has been for many years. Autumns have come and gone — milestones have been passed—and the gun barks no more. It has resigned itself to the golden rule of "Live and let live."

I remember the happy hunting season when we were invited by some old friends to their big farm. For us it was almost like a homecoming; it was a friendship we cherished. Just to hike through the fields on a beautiful, warm autumn day with its clear blue skies, to smell the fragrance of the newly-tilled soil and to feel the gentle breeze rustling through the cornstalks, was an experience to anticipate almost rapturously. I still remember the lunch brought to us in the field. A real treat it was: fresh fried chicken, sandwiches from newly-baked homemade bread, coffee and a big triangle of blueberry pie. There was autumn tranquility in that carefree world. No rush, no hurry, not a breath of pressure. Time stood still. Unforgettable memories!

The hunting was good and the pheasants were healthy, fat and abundant. Those were the golden years! It is too bad they could not last. In the late '40s, Minnesota had millions of healthy and strong pheasants and they were crowing, flying and running in all directions. All along the roads, birds were picking sand and gravel. It was a sight to behold for all lovers of wildlife. In fact, some of the farmers were so happy to see the city hunters coming out to harvest some of the surplus birds. It was really a bumper crop in those years. And they came three hundred thousand strong, men, women and boys; anybody that could walk through a cornfield or carry a gun was present. That was not any ordinary hunting tribe of gentlemanly behavior. It was like a mob army invasion on the move. They swarmed all over farms and fields with total disregard of the owner or the man who was farming the land, and to ask permission to hunt was seldom done. If a farmer had posted a "No Hunting" sign on his property, it was an insult to the hunting tribe. They ran over the land, through farmyards and fences. Just ease the automobile bumper up to the fencepost, push it down and drive into the field. It was the wildest bunch of people that went hunting or handled a gun. Some of the most aggressive would even go tramping through the farmyard and shoot calves, hens and ducks. Often the shooting was so wild that the farmer and his family had to hide in the basement.

Sometimes there would be as many as eighteen men walking through the cornfield side by side; when a bird flew up, all eighteen guns would start barking. It sounded like a war and the pellets converged into the mark. Often the pheasant was so mutilated by the pellets before it hit the ground that there was hardly a feather left. All had a grand time shooting and laughing and swigging at the bottle. The sharpshooters were posted at the end of the field because the birds were running ahead of the walking men and, of course, to escape, the pheasants had to fly over the hunters at that point and here they really poured it on. It did not take very long before every hunter had his limit, from six to eight birds in possession. Of course, the shooting did not stop at that. It was too much fun and besides they had too many birds to drag home in the bag, so the small birds were dumped out, and from then on, only a big rooster would be picked up.

In the evening when everybody was home-bound, the traffic became very slow moving; it was bumper-to-bumper. The highway patrol was regulating the traffic in the highway fork where the road from the west merged with one from the north. It took some time, with many stops, and of course after dark everybody thought it was the game warden's checking point, and all the hunters with extra birds had to get rid of those that were over the limit. So the birds were thrown into the ditch. The next morning the newspaper could report that three truckloads of pheasants were picked up at this fork in the two highways. According to hundreds of farmers and also many gentlemen hunters, there were thousands of dead pheasant hens left to rot in the fields, and often the stench from the dead birds was so overwhelming that the farmer had to plow the birds under to get rid of the terrible smell.

For years it has been mysterious how the citizens of this country could accomplish the impossible—kill uncounted millions of wild animals and birds in the very short time of 250 years. But after I had witnessed the butchering of the pheasants in the late forties and early fifties, now I know it could easily be done. And it was a repeating of that performance that had utterly extinguished the buffaloes and the passenger pigeons, the prairie chickens and many more animals which were senselessly slaughtered and destroyed. Now the pheasants have disappeared like the rest of our fauna. Empty and lonesome are the cornfields, and the wonderful crowing of a pheasant rooster in early spring is now just about a thing of the past. So many people are wondering what happened to the millions of pheasants. Of course, it can be blamed on many things but we must not forget the inevitable rule: if the backbone of a species is broken, it seldom can be nursed back to a healthy population. And if we are going to have any luck in restoring our wildlife we must learn to like our fellow travelers on this earth, and treat them well.

But so far this has never been practiced in the United States of America.

Some people are trying to find the reason for the disappearance of the pheasants. Certain groups believe that there is insufficient food left in the fields after the harvest, because agricultural methods and machinery have been tremendously improved. The birds starve to death. Other people point out that the pheasants cannot obtain the sand necessary to their lives because of the increased area of hard-surfaced roads. Then also there are those who blame the foxes for killing the birds and this might seem to be indicated by the reports that pheasant carcasses have been found in fox dens.

However, in addition to these possible causes, we must not forget the unprecedented evolution in farming today. Every year the farmers spray thousands of tons of weed-killing poisons in the fields and in any place where weeds grow. It destroys the weeds and also all the life in that region. Nothing can live and reproduce in a poisonous environment. We should know that. The report that many pheasant carcasses are found in foxes' dens seems to prove that the foxes are killing off the birds. However, before we jump to that conclusion, we must know if the pheasants were strong and healthy or if they were half dead, poisoned by food that they had picked up. That is a very important question.

When people begin to destroy normal life in nature, the link is broken and a chain of reaction takes place. The poison will kill off the field mice, gophers, chipmunks, squirrels and rabbits. When they are dead and gone, what are the foxes supposed to live on? If the farmer kills off all the rodents and all the foxes, will he then have found the answer to enormous crops, wealth and happiness? Or would we have enormous hordes of grasshoppers, locusts and worms that would consume all the green leaves on every tree? The bugs would come swarming in as they did in the dark years. Of course, we have the ammunition to kill all intruders. We can spread poison on thousands of acres from airplanes, but we must remember that poison accumulates on the fields and it will reach to a point of total sterilization where nothing will grow at all. And we must not only think about the sterile result today, but about what will happen next year or in the following years. And this poison is the most dreaded, deadly chemical the human race has ever produced and it could be our death, doom and dreadful Judgment Day.

I have in the last years made an interesting experiment in observing our wildlife in their natural environment. Our home, a small estate, is located in the city of Bloomington, Minnesota. It consists of 70 acres of high wooded hills, deep ravines, a small stream, and a good-sized, man-made lake. The lake is 150 feet wide, approximately half a mile long and about fifteen feet deep. When the lake is finally completed it will have a two-and-one-half-acre island in the center, where pheasants and ducks will have their refuge.

At present the rich soil and foliage around the lake makes a haven for all the small rodents, including muskrats and beavers. The woods with its big old trees is a home for red and grey squirrels, chipmunks, beavers, raccoons, foxes and deer. There are numerous species of birds ranging from tiny creepers to pheasants, from dull-looking sparrows to the brilliant-colored cardinals and bluejays, flashing like rubies and sapphires. In different places around the lake and in the woods are feeding stations for all these happy free-loaders. My plan is to feed pheasants and Hungarian partridges during the winter. All the woodland's creatures like nothing better than to help themselves at the feeding stations. Even the foxes when they are hungry enough, eat corn, and also meat trimmings and scraps from the meat locker.

My observation during the last three years is that if the snow is not heavy, foxes will hunt field mice, gophers and rabbits and not kill the pheasants. Only when the snow is too deep for the rodents will the foxes hunt pheasants, and these are not from the regular flock but mostly loners, maybe an old male that was chased out by the younger ones. As far as I have observed, the killing seems to occur toward evening when the pheasants are ready to roost in the trees. However, when the snow has melted down and the small rodents come to the surface, the pheasant killing stops.

Of course, this is only a small project, but it is quite interesting because the pheasant population has increased in the three years quite remarkably, and it will continue to do so providing the snipers will leave them alone.

THE INTRUDER—COTTONTAILS　　　　　　　　　　　　　　　　　　　　　　　　　Collection of Wildlife of America

Trapping Wild Animals

Since the earliest times, in the long tale of the human race, trappers have used horrible devices for trapping wild animals with no thought at all about the humanitarian side of this occupation. The main purpose in trapping was to catch and hold the animal until the hunter came and killed it. In many countries today there still exists the so-called pitfall as a silent witness to the hunter's cruel treatment of wildlife. It is a hole dug in field or forest, from five to eight feet deep and quite short so that there is no chance for the animal to take off, to give a spring or leap in order to escape.

The pit was camouflaged on the top with wood branches, twigs and grass, so that the animal was unaware of the hole before it and tumbled in. Often in the bottom of the pit there was a pointed wooden post standing in the ground to impale the falling animal. The poor creature would literally be hanging on the post as he died a slow, terrible death.

Maybe the worst part was the actual killing of the trapped animal. It was unbelievably gruesome. The animal was clubbed, speared, knifed or stoned to death. Often a pitfall was forgotten by those who made it. Maybe the hunter moved to another territory, or forgot where the hole was. In many of these pitfalls are to be found the bones of animals that starved to death.

We have made a little progress in our relations with wild animals. Today the pitfall is prohibited by law in most civilized countries. But in this country we allow traps made of steel and iron that are just as barbarous as pitfalls, causing unspeakable anguish to their victims. In many towns and villages in the United States, there are hunters' and trappers' museums, often rich collections of animal traps and hunting gear. These are sagas in steel, blood and iron, condemning evidence of our brutal dealings with our wildlife, proof of our disregard of God's creatures and our fellow-travelers on this earth.

The most common trap is the steel animal trap, the worst of them all. In European countries, the steel trap is outlawed. When the animal steps on a center trigger, the trap snaps shut on a leg or paw and the animal is locked in a steel jaw. The trap has a steel chain that can be fastened to a tree or log. Sometimes the leg is paralyzed or frozen, and the animal will chew his own leg off to free himself. It is because of this that we have so many animals limping around on three legs in our fields and forests. Many steel traps are set by unscrupulous people who forget them. In such cases, one is apt to find later a part of a front leg still locked in the trap, or a skeleton beside it. One of our wild creatures has paid the supreme penalty in a world of greedy, heartless people who call themselves civilized.

The time has come to take a sober look at this situation in our woods and on the prairies. It is so quiet, so dead there! It is not as it was many years ago. Then our woods were teeming with animals and birds. They were flying, crawling and galloping in all directions. It was a wonderful experience to witness the life and activity. Now that is all a thing of the past. A person can walk miles and miles in the woods and never see anything bigger than a squirrel or rabbit. Even those friendly little creatures are seldom seen.

In the old days a hike in the forest after a fresh snowfall was a journey of immense discovery, an open book in which the members of our wildlife left their footprints, a criss-cross of trails and patterns through the woods and fields. It was an interesting experience to try and identify the tracks of the different species.

But that is a thing of the sad, faraway past. The present generation will never have that wonderful fun of reading footprints. No, the book of snow will lie there shining white, unauthored by living creatures. The new fresh snow will pretend to cover up the tracks that are not there. Mother Nature again opens her book of snow, welcoming her small creatures to print their tracks on her bediamonded page, waiting and wondering. But she must wait a long time. And she does not know that many of her children will never come back.

THE ELK

The Thomas D. Murphy Company

The Trophy Hunter

The dinner was over in the big, sprawling mansion. The ladies drifted into the long living room and the men, with their pipes and cigars lighted, wandered into the den, a combination of library and hobby room. A fire was burning. It was warm and cozy. On the long wall there was row after row of wild animal heads — trophies collected as far away as the Arctic Circle and the darkest Africa. The proud owner, the great wild animal hunter, loved to show off and describe his great struggles—his heroic fight against those wild beasts. On a low chair in front of the fireplace his sixteen-year-old son George sat listening. He was slenderly built, with a fair complexion, blue eyes and a charming smile. The father was describing the terrible ordeal with the great bull moose from Alaska, his latest trophy. The horn spread was only one and a half inches less than the world's record. The great hunter's story about the struggle poured out as he told about the mighty river he had to cross, the lowlands and swamps he had to slosh through, the steep hills he had to crawl up, and the cold nights when he slept in a snowbank.

The next morning he started on the trail again after the mighty trophy. His provisions ran out the third day of the chase, but he was luckly enough to shoot a caribou. He cut off a piece of meat and fried it over a small fire. It tasted wonderful. The fourth morning, the moose was all tired out. The great hunter crawled on his stomach for a half mile. His hands were nearly frozen. Then he finally got close enough to fire a shot, he was shaking so that he could hardly hold the rifle still. The powerful rifle barked, the shot was a little high, so that the wounded bull turned and came charging toward him, the big legs going like piston rods, the head bent, those magnificent horns ready to pick him up, toss him into the air and then trample him to death. But he was lucky. When the moose was only ten yards away, the rifle barked again and the big bull tumbled over dead only a yard or two away. Then, for the first time he felt cold and hungry and he didn't know what to do. Finally, he got out his big hunting knife, cut the bull's throat and drank the warm blood. That gave him warmth and his strength came back.

Then a mighty storm came up. He could not see an arm's length away. He was so cold his hands were numb. Again he was the great hunter who knew what to do. He cut the moose's stomach open, pulled out the guts and crawled inside the moose, where he slept all night.

The next morning, the sun was shining. It was quite warm. He cut off the big trophy's head, and after three days of hiking, carrying the moose's head with him, he reached the camp.

George was sitting, listening. He noticed that some of the men did not quite believe the whole story by the way they winked at each other, but he himself thought it was terrific. The only trouble was that George was with his dad when he shot the big moose and the true story differed some from that which the dinner guests heard. First the great trophy hunter had hired an airplane and a helicopter. The airplane, equipped with skis, could land on snow and ice, even in an emergency. The helicopter was used to locate the moose herds and to spot the big specimens. It was on the second day that they found the one with the magnificent shovel horns, and it was shot right from the helicopter. The pilot and the guide cut off the big head, washed away the blood, put a cellophane bag over the cut and lifted the head into the airplane.

George looked at the great hunter. A sympathetic smile passed over the young face as he thought, "Poor Dad! He lives in a world of a thousand years ago! He is the great hunter from the Stone Age, dressed in skins fastened over his shoulder. In one hand he carries a stone club, in the other he drags a big moose by the horns. He is the great hunter, the superb provider for the whole tribe!"

Years have rolled by, the great trophy hunter is no more. On his gravestone is carved the day and year he was born, the date of his death and "Rest in Peace." In winter when the snow swirls over the grave, circling the stone monument, a little bank forms on the lea side, and little by little the carving is covered over with snow.

His son is now a grown man and is the new master of the sprawling mansion. His wife demands to know what he is going to do with those horrible things on the wall in the library, wondering with impatience why he can not give those heads to somebody. So he telephones everybody he can think of, but the answer is "No," always "No."

Some time later an automobile with a trailer behind rolls slowly out toward open country. The trailer is thoroughly covered by a tarpaulin. What is underneath is nobody's business. George turns in where the sign says, "City Dump." The man in charge is burning some wooden boxes and has a big fire blazing. George backs the trailer toward the flames and head after head is thrown into the fire.

As George stands gazing at those flames licking the great trophies, he is thinking, "Soon they will all crumble to ashes. The dust will fly and disappear over the landscape and the last memory of the meaningless project will be gone forever. What a waste of time and money and energy, the silly residue of great destructiveness and vanity! If all the big game animals in our wilderness are killed for trophies then only the small ones will remain of our once beautiful wild animals."

The Meat Hunter

The game hunters of the world can be classified into five kinds: (1) the meat hunter, (2) the nuisance hunter, (3) the bow-and-arrow hunter, (4) the trophy hunter, (a) the brown bear hunter, (b) the polar bear hunter, and (5) the sports hunter. Each will be described.

The meat hunter is the most common and also the oldest kind of hunter in the world. He has not changed much from the cave-dwelling days when the only source of food was wild animals and birds. He has no interest in the beauty of the land and sky or the graceful animals and the colorful birds. For him a hike in God's country on a beautiful fall day has little attraction. His object is meat and only meat. He has his license: it is paid for and he has a legal right to his kill. The minute the season opens, he is ready and eager to fire the first shot. He must get his prey as soon as possible. If he is hunting deer—and luck is with him—he throws the deer on top of his car and is homeward bound. Then he cuts up the meat, puts it into the freezer, washes the blood from his hands, and he is through for the year.

If he does not get his deer or birds, he will howl long and loud and blame everybody for the poor results. For him the hunting season is not at all an adventure or recreation, only a day's work. Often among a flock of meat hunters, a small war is fought over a newly killed deer when two parties claim ownership. It is not so long ago in one deer hunting season in Minnesota that eighteen men were shot to death, nineteen died of heart failure and eight died of suffocation in trailers. (And we call deer hunting a healthy recreation!)

The name "meat hunter" is a term now frowned upon in the civilized world because he is no longer the big hero, the great hunter, the brave provider, the "bringing-home-the-bacon" man.

Why should the meat hunter be condemned? Is it his fault that nobody has taught him the sensible way to hunt? Throughout his life he has seen and heard only the killing-shooting-trapping theme song: "Get your limit first before the next fellow. Get it now. It might be gone tomorrow." Would not the meat hunter be a different man and see and do things in a different way, if from his boyhood he had learned the unwritten law of the wilderness? He would have a richer life and wider horizon and know the important rules of conservation.

The Polar Bear Hunter

The small, fast twin-engine plane left the Seattle Airport by daybreak and headed north over Puget Sound, skirted the west boundary of British Columbia, followed the Alaskan coastline north over Wales Island across Russell Fjord, then inland over the endless Alaskan wilderness. Lake and river shimmered in the morning sun. A nice town, still asleep, and lonely farms and cabins nestled in this tremendously big timberland. Over the hills and mountains were layers of blue haze covering the rugged country and in the lowland, light fog was slowly lifting in the morning breeze. Mount McKinley, with its white top, looked like a statue of shining marble, a landmark in all this wilderness. Some hours later the plane dipped down at an airport for refueling and an overnight stop. The next morning they took off again and headed north, crossing the Arctic Circle and in over the bare tundra.

Mack Hudson, the sponsor of this big game, big trophy expedition, was a young man with lots of money, a get-rich-quick fellow with lots of luck and ambition. However, Mack had come to the conclusion that there are some things in this world money cannot buy — friendship, prestige and admiration. He had many friends, but Mack knew the difference between "friendship" and "acquaintance." Sure, he had some old friends whom he had known for many years, but there were others who hung around just because of his money. Mack had made up his mind that he was going to amount to something—something great—so that people would look up to him as an outstanding personality. An old friend suggested that he take up big game hunting, that he be a leader of an expedition for big trophies, and bring home some record trophies for folks to see and admire. Well, Mack was not stupid. He knew that to hunt for great trophies was an outstanding achievement many years ago—people didn't know any better. Nowadays the human race has found that many of our wild animals make excellent pets, so the glory of big game hunting has worn pretty thin. Although Mack loved animals and birds, he decided to take a swing at it anyway. He was one of those fellows who, if he had decided to do something, it must be all or nothing.

Mack was on his way to the Arctic to hunt polar bears. He knew exactly the size of the record head, and his must be the biggest of the big. Mack had studied the saga of the wide wilderness to learn where the big ones were to be found. His airplane was the best that money could buy and the pilot was famous for his flights in the polar regions. In the plane, there was superior hunting equipment and enough food for two men for three weeks' stay, if necessary. He couldn't miss! It was springtime in the Arctic, with small and large lakes forming from the melting snow, blinking like mirrors in the sun. Over the hills and meadows, the green grass was like a carpet covering the landscape; and often through the lingering snow cover, the wild flowers were peeking. Great herds of caribou were on the move north to the tundra. It was amazing that they could find food on the barren land and that they could endure the swarm of mosquitoes, often so thick that they shadowed the sun.

Some of the birds were still in flight northward, but thousands and thousands were already there. In Amundsen Gulf there was open water and farther north big ice floes were on the move. Once in a while, as the plane dipped low, the men looked for polar bears which were few and far between. Farther north where the ice was more compact, they found a place to land. The landing was a tricky operation because of the high landing speed, but the pilot was an expert. He banked and fishtailed the plane to reduce the landing speed. He skimmed only a few feet above the ice. The skis went down and touched the frozen surface. It was smooth but the runway was too short, so a new approach was made by starting the slowdown of the flight farther back. This time the plane had enough room and they settled down.

The pilot had spent many years in and out of the Arctic. He could not explain it, but this silent, majestic white wilderness was always calling him back. It was a kind of craving that he could not resist. He had seen the polar night in the springtime, an unforgettable beauty, a dreamland so enchanting, like a great symphony in color and light. He had traveled far and wide in many lands, had seen many beautiful sights, but they could not compare with this gloriously silent ice plateau. The landscape was varied, for there was not any solid form or shape. The ice and the light blended perfectly in a mellow twilight over the horizon. The stars in splendid brightness twinkled in the clear air, each one like a great lantern in heaven's enormous kingdom. Sometimes the northern lights, in silver glitter, sent flames that crackled and flung long arches of blazing rainbow colors in a fantastic dance over the endless horizon. The pilot had often wondered about all this beauty, so generously displayed in this faraway land, a place that so few of the earth's souls have a chance to enjoy and admire, this unforgettable, frozen north.

They pitched their tent on a big ice floe. The pilot, an excellent cook, served a delicious meal. They enjoyed sitting outside the tent. Afterward they crawled on top of the plane for a better panoramic view. They did not speak. It was not necessary. The blue smoke from their pipes drifted in the clear air. The midnight sun, still on the lower horizon, sent a warm glow over the high ice mountains that were drifting southward in the far distance. Time passed. It was midnight, the start of a new day, twilight over the polar region. They could not sleep because there was too much to see and admire, and besides, nobody could sleep in all that light.

Some hours later they took off and headed north over the vast plateau. The terrain was rough with high-top dikes made by drifting ice floes crashing against the solid ice floors in storms. The farther north they went, the rougher the plateau was. They turned east and found open water with drifting ice floes and also some seals and polars bears. They circled the area to find a large enough landing strip, not too far from the open water. After some exploring they decided that a landing strip would be much better if it were closer to the hunting ground. Consequently, the next day they moved to their new site where they pitched camp. The weather was still fairly warm, and there followed unforgettable days and nights.

One evening Mack decided to take a hike in the direction of the open water. He had his gun with him in case he should see some large bears. He soon was beside the open water, walking slowly and carefully, stepping over many large and small cracks in the ice. If he should fall, it would certainly be the end. Mack was enjoying the walk when suddenly he spotted a big polar bear behind an ice block. He could see only the head, neck and shoulders but the bear looked large and broad—it must be a big one.

The bear did not move—he lay with his back toward Mack and seemed to be sound asleep. Mack was creeping low, sliding on his stomach to get in the right position for a good shot. He knew that the bullet must strike the vertebra for instant death. Even a shot through the head would never kill a polar bear outright. The bear might attack the hunter or maybe dive into the water. Mack was crawling over a small ice chunk where he had a chance to rest the rifle for a steady aim. He estimated the range at 75 meters. The rifle aim-site found the shoulder blades and moved along the neck toward the big head. There the movement stopped and the rifle moved down to the center of the big neck. Mack squeezed the trigger. The gun barked. The big head jerked up a little, then dropped down and lay still. All was quiet as before. Only the rifle crack, the shattering noise, had disturbed the wilderness' peaceful repose.

Somehow, Mack felt the explosion did not belong in this wonderful region. He walked slowly over to where the bear was lying, his gun ready in case the bear was still alive. Some blood from the bullet hole in the neck was dribbling down on the ice forming a big red rose in the pure white snow. As he got closer, he froze in his tracks, for he saw a young bear cub, quite small, feeding, pushing, sucking on the nipples, trying to get more milk where there was none. The cub sat up and looked straight at Mack, wondering where the figure came from. For Mack, it certainly was a great shot. He was supposed to be a big game hunter, the famous trophy collector, and here, lo and behold, he had killed a mama bear with a small cub! It was certainly a good thing that nobody had witnessed this terrible ordeal. The only thing he could do now was to shoot the cub, drag the carcass over to the open water and slide it in. The rifle was aimed at the little fellow, but Mack hesitated. He saw the innocent, white, roly-poly teddy bear with black nose and eyes, so handsome and adorable. How could anybody have the heart to kill him, a royal prince from the kingdom of the North Pole? No, Mack could not destroy him. He would have to talk things over with the pilot. He would certainly know what to do.

It turned out to be a long night, listening to the cub crying. It finally fell asleep for a while, but not for long. The men felt sorry for him. If there were only something they could do! As Mack lay awake, listening, he thought about this strange land with its saga of snow and ice. He had read so many stories about the polar expeditions and their struggles toward the north — sailing, rowing, pushing and pulling their equipment with determination, energy and hope. These were stouthearted men, rime-covered in their bulky clothes, ghostlike figures in blowing snowstorms, men in steady movement forward, their eyes searching north—always north in a never-giving-up hope.

In the last hundred years so many of the North Pole expeditions reached the end of their trail with disaster and death. Hunger, frost, sickness and long, cold and dark Arctic winter drained their energy and strength and dimmed their hope. Many had reached the borderline of the impossible. When the end of the trail was reached it was a long, long way back. They retreated like soldiers in a war they had lost, wandering back as beaten men, with hunger, frost and sickness taking its great toll. Often they stumbled forward in their harness in front of the sleds and died with their faces in the snow. Many a shallow grave was chipped in the ice with a cross as a marker and a little snow on top of the grave.

The last man of an expedition of 135, the only one left, was sitting on an ice block, his head in his hands. An Eskimo woman spoke to him. He lifted his head and looked at her. In his eyes there was a hopeless gleam from the soul's deepest sorrow. Then he tumbled over and died.

Why did these men leave home and a secure life in exchange for this endless struggle in a strange, unfriendly polar region with its blustering winter cold and raging snowstorms? Maybe it is as the great Norwegian explorer Dr. Fridtjof Nansen wrote: "Have you known the great white silence? Have you broken trail on snowshoes? Mushed your huskies up the rivers? Dared the unknown? Led the way and clutched the prize? Have you suffered, starved and triumphed? Groveled down, yet grasped the glory? Done things just for the doing, letting babblers tell the story— the simple things, the true things, the silent men who do things? Then listen to the wild, it is calling you. Let us journey to a lonely land I know. There is a whisper in the night wind, there is a star agleam to guide us. The wild is calling. Let us go!"

Mack listened to the lonely, blue sea gull sailing free and light, soaring on outstretched wings over the immense wilderness. The bird's sorrowful, lonely flute call belonged here. It was like an echo of the explorer's cry from those who struggled and died in the winter land's ice, snow and unmerciful cold.

It was high noon on the ice floe and there was not much of a change in the situation. The cub had consumed a can of tuna fish and some milk. It seemed to give him more strength to cry out louder and louder. Twice he had wandered off to look for his mother, disappeared for a time, but he always came back to the camp. As Mack stood in the door of the plane, he spotted a white object coming toward the camp. He followed its progress and soon it was apparent that a polar bear was coming for a visit. The pilot took one look and decided they had better get out of camp in a hurry, for a polar bear could be quite mean at times. To move the camp in such a rush would be impossible, so they decided to stay to welcome the bear. Of course, it is a common fact that often the male polar bear will try to kill the young ones if he has a chance.

The men talked things over. If the bear tried to kill the cub, they would have to shoot it. Then how about the cub? Would they take him along home and give him to a zoo where he would be put in a small enclosure for the rest of his life? They had visited many zoos and always felt sorry for those poor animals in the cages. Some visitors to the zoo were often cruel to the poor animals who had to spend their lives so far removed from their natural environment. It is unbelievable that human beings—supposedly civilized—could find pleasure in torturing these innocent creatures.

The bear was not wasting any time. The ten-foot-high dikes were no obstacle to it. It traveled fast and alone. Mack and the pilot crawled on top of the plane and had their rifles ready. They left the cub on the ice so that the bear would not damage the plane if it were after the cub. The bear came closer, snorting and growling. The frightened cub took refuge behind an ice block. He looked so cute, standing on his hind legs and peeking over the block.

Stopping a short distance from the plane, the bear took its time in looking over the layout. Then it lifted its great head and took the scent, approaching slowly, not sure what to expect with all those contraptions in front of it. The airplane had its greatest interest—smelling at the wings, walking around looking, moving to the tent and looking in. The cub, in the meantime, had followed the whole proceedings with great interest. He had not opened his mouth, not a sound. The bear in the tent had found some bread and other food which it consumed in a hurry. It walked out on the ice where it soon got the scent of the cub. It walked slowly over to the little fellow who stood there so frightened, trying to get away. The big bear put its paw on him and held him down. Two rifles were pointed at the bear, with fingers on the triggers, watching and waiting.

The bear smelled the cub all over. It was in no hurry. After a long time, it sat down on the ice and with its front paws, in a long sweeping movement, gathered in the cub and tucked him to its stomach. All was silent—only a happy squeak from the cub. The men looked at each other smiling and then they laughed out loud. Some time later the cub and his foster-mother went on their way toward the open fjord.

During this expedition, Mack and the pilot sealed a friendship pact which lasted for years. The pilot often visits Mack's home where he admires the wonderful collection in the trophy room. Now they are not heads of dead animals, but some excellent paintings, framed and hanging on the walls, the work of a promising young artist in the United States. Every year in early summer an airplane with two men aboard leaves the Seattle Airport and heads north toward the quiet and peaceful wilderness. The polar region is in their blood.

THE MULE DEER
The Thomas D. Murphy Company

Joe the Deer Hunter

Joe had for the first time in many years not been able to go deer hunting. He had too many things to do and now it was the last day of the hunting season. During the summer and fall he had noticed a place out in the woods where three does and a magnificent buck with horns big enough to be a seven-pointer, were hanging around, and he was sure that they were still there.

He piloted his brand-new car slowly and carefully out toward the woods. He must not drive too fast and recklessly for the first few hundred miles—so the instructions said. The new car was for Joe his pride and joy in life. To have a new car every year means a lot of prestige and also so much respect and admiration for people with old worn-out clunks. A new auto was for Joe a craving he could not resist. For him it was a must.

The next Sunday he would be going to church, driving the new automobile right up to the church entrance, taking a long time to open the door for his wife to get out and then helping her up the many steps. It would give the church folks a chance to gaze and admire this brand-new, shining car with all those fancy extras. Then he would drive the car slowly and carefully to the parking lot, hanging around for a little while. There might be some fellows out there who would like to look at this wonderful miracle. He knew that that day in church he would not be able to listen to the sermon or take part in the singing. His thoughts would be with the new precious car out in the parking lot.

If only he would be lucky enough to get a big buck it certainly would help him in many ways. The payments on the new car were pretty big, and then there were all those other bills that must be paid every month. Of course, he was not complaining about the automobile's installments. Joe was not thinking about those bills today. He was in the driver's seat, the motor purring like a contented cat and the smell inside the car was for Joe the most wonderful perfume in the whole world. Besides, he could gaze at all those fascinating instrument push-buttons, switches and gadgets. It looked like the instrument panel of a big airplane. He was as happy as a lucky boy on Christmas morning.

He reached the woods and parked the car in an open place beside the road to be sure that nobody would hit the precious car or sideswipe it. It was a cold day and the wind came sweeping over the open fields. Some snowflakes were swirling in the air. Winter was coming. Joe opened the trunk and pulled out a horsehide, red-brown in color, big and warm. He put the fur hide over the hood and the radiator, tucking it tender-heartedly in and around like a mother tucking her child in bed. It would keep the motor warm and make it easy to start. Then he grabbed his rifle, stepped over the fence and long-legged and husky, with long steps, he was heading into the woods.

He was sure that now the deer were bedded down in the small ravine where the buck would always stand guard on the top. He must circle through the woods, walk against the wind so the deer could not catch the scent of him at some distance and move on. It was a long way around with many twists and turns, thick underbrush that he had to get through and also there were many grapevines to entangle him. Then he came to the big creek and he had to find a place where he could step across.

Well, he found that he had spent too much time and presently he was not sure in what direction he was walking. The sun was not out and he was all mixed up. He could not tell if he was traveling north or south. He could not find the deer or the ravine. He was lost and worried. His new car was out there somewhere. But where? The dusk comes early in November. It seemed to be seeping into the woods, and after dusk comes the twilight. And then the darkness set in.

Now he was really worried. He increased the length of his steps and also the tempo. He was rambling and hastening through the woods like a crazy man. Some time later, he began to follow a fence and he figured that the fence must lead to a farm and there he could ask directions from the farm folks. He followed the fence for some time and finally he was out in the open. Thank heaven! No more woods to hamper him. Out in the open there was more light. He sure was glad that he found the fence and followed it.

Coming over a small ridge, he stopped. He got all excited because only two hundred yards away stood his buck. This day was certainly the luckiest in all his life! He lifted the rifle. The outline of the buck was not very clear but he could see the big horns, so all that he had to do was to move the rifle back and down a little to fire a shoulder shot. The gun barked. The buck still stood. He did not move. Joe must have missed that one. Now he knelt down on one knee for a more steady shot. The gun barked once more. The buck still stood there like a statue. Joe had heard some fantastic stories about a hunter that shot a deer stone-dead, but which was still standing. It was as though the deer had been frozen solid so that the hunter had to give it a push first and then tumble it over.

Joe knew for certain that this most unusual thing had now happened to him also. It was unbelievable! Of course, he could have just stunned the buck, so he better fire another shot to be sure. Close by was a tree. Joe moved over, put the rifle barrel against the tree trunk for a most painstaking, steady aim. He fired the third shot. Nothing happened. Then walking down the small ridge, he followed a dry creek bed, and ducked through some thick underbrush. Then he walked to the top of the creek bank. He froze in his tracks. Because, only a few yards away stood his precious possession. It gurgled water from the cylinder block and the radiator, and through the horsehide and the hood were three big bullet holes! In front of the car there stood a tree six feet high, dry and withered with a few branches sticking out. Yep! That was the big buck's rack horns that Joe was looking at!

THE SMALLMOUTH BASS

The Thomas D. Murphy Company

The Happy Wanderer

Hank Lee left his car at the wilderness landing and packed his camping equipment on his back. From the landing there were hiking trails fanning out in all directions. He was back again after four long years, back to the wilderness, to the land of his dreams and longing! He had his sleeping bag, his tent, cooking utensils and food enough for a whole week. Besides, he had his fishing rod—he could live off the land if he had to.

Yes, he was back from the service—after four years in strange and crowded lands, back from the dirt and filth so common in those parts of the world. But all that was forgotten. He was the happy wanderer, whistling a happy tune, always whistling when he walked. To have been away for four years seemed a very long time, but he had never forgotten this wonderful trail between lustrous, green, tall trees, past the shimmering blue lakes, over stones and moss-grown paths, over hills with a sweeping view of gorgeous land. This magnificent wilderness with its lakes, rivers and streams—even though it had been a long time to wait, at last he was back.

It was some hours ago that he left the landing. He was not in any hurry. There were too many things to see and admire, with a good rest now and then in the cool of the morning. He headed for a small creek between two big lakes, a perfect place for a vacation and rest.

When he reached a bend in the trail just before the brook, he stopped, put his hand behind his ear, mouth open, listening. A warm smile glided over his face. He nodded a couple of times. Yes, he could hear his old friend, the small, bubbling, laughing, mumbling creek. The brook's voice changed, sometimes it sounded as though it were scolding. Hank ran the last few steps, threw his camping gear on the ground and leaped down to the creek's shore. He lay down on his stomach, put both hands solidly on the bottom of the cold, clear brook and felt the sand and gravel under his hands, also the rippling water over his face —cooling, soothing. He took sip after sip of the God-given streaming water. There had been four years of burning thirst in his soul for this opportunity.

After a while he crawled back to the grass and the moss-covered flat ground and lay there looking at the clouds drifting slowly in the sunny summer sky. This was not a dream. He was actually here again quenching his thirst from this pure, clear creek, from this wonderful stream. He had traveled in many lands. He remembered so many places in the world — villages where the slimy, stinking water ran through streets in dug ditches, and big cities where rivers were not clean. No, the water was dark-brown with filthy stuff floating in it; even dead cats and rats were drifting past. He remembered the smoke-filled, dirty restaurants offering water, evil-smelling from greasy-looking glasses. He remembered the hot burning sun in the dusty desert. All through that long ordeal he was always dreaming about his wonderful friend, the sparkling clean, laughing brook offering him water, the most precious thing in the world.

After a tasty lunch he took a rest and fell sound asleep. When he finally woke up, the sun was setting. He pitched his tent, fried a fish he had caught and had his evening meal in company with his cheerful friend. Afterwards, he went for a long hike in this glorious land. He was not in any hurry. There were so many things to see and enjoy.

When he returned to the camp, he sat outside his tent smoking. The night's mellow darkness crept slowly in, covering the landscape. Only the brook's mumbling, soothing sound was heard through the peaceful wilderness.

Two days later he went fishing to the upper lake. He followed the creek for some time, then took a shortcut to the lake and found a small landing where the lake water flowed into the creek. It seemed like a good place to try his fishing luck. He got his rod ready and started casting across the narrow stream. Some time later he discovered a big sign near the shore line. He figured that it must be some instruction for canoe travelers. Crossing the narrows to get a better look at the sign, he read: *"DANGER! WATER POLLUTED! CONTAMINATED! UNFIT FOR HUMAN CONSUMPTION! DON'T DRINK IT!"*

He laughed out loud. Some joker must have erected that sign in the wilderness, here where the cleanest, purest water in the world was to be found, here in the deep wilderness. He started fishing again, but he could not get the sign out of his mind.

Then he stopped fishing. He remembered a letter he had received from Stanley, his partner on a fishing trip here four years ago. The letter informed him that three big lakes and streams in the wilderness had been tested and found to be polluted. He did not believe it at the time. It was a shocking report. Unbelievable!

He looked at the water flowing into the creek. His friend! The model for all pure sparkling water in the world, the laughing brook, the stream he had loved in all his dreams when he was in those far-off, lonely places of the world! Then anger gripped him. He pounded his clenched fist in the air, he shouted out loud: "No, no, no! Not my creek! No! No! You dirty, filthy swine!"

He sat down on a big rock, his head in his hands. How could this unbelievable thing have happened? He looked over at the beautiful blue lake. He thought of how the water from this lake would flow into others like a cancer in the body, spreading to others. Soon the whole region would be infected. Then there would be signs all over the wilderness: *Polluted water! Danger! Don't Drink It!* How can people be so dirty, so careless? Don't we have any laws to guard our wilderness? Can *anybody* destroy our beautiful lakes? How about the younger generation? Their heritage? If this thing had happened in those backward countries, where people do not know any better and cannot afford to take precautions, then maybe it would be excusable. But here in America, the richest country in the world! Why do we dump everything into lakes and rivers?

He wandered back to his tent, took it down, packed his equipment and was ready to leave. He was looking and listening to the brook. It did not bubble or laugh any more. Sorrowful, it sounded lonely, deceived, neglected, it looked cheated as a member of the wilderness that it was!

Hank was not the happy wanderer any more. He did not recognize the shimmering lakes and rippling streams. He walked like a man who had lost the most precious thing in the world; his dream had crumbled. He found the key to the car's trunk, lifted the cover and dumped in the camping gear. When he closed the cover, he noticed the license plate on his car with its slogan: "10,000 Lakes."

He stood for some time looking at the plate, thinking: "Ten thousand blue shimmering lakes, pure and irreplaceable. Jewels! Priceless treasures to any country in the world. They soon will be cesspools with evil-smelling water."

NIGHT WATCH—RACCOONS Collection of Wildlife of America

Todde the Raccoon

It was Christmas Eve. Quiet and peaceful lay the landscape in a world of fresh, soft snow. The old oak tree, standing so big and sturdy, still clung to a few of last summer's leaves, now dry and brown. It was truly a beautiful winter scene, decorated for the holidays in white and brown.

The pale December sun flickered over the hill, the deep forest and the lowlands. Distant church bells were ringing, their deep sounds vibrating through the invigorating air.

From the dark ravine came the incessant barking of Veslemor, a young Norwegan elghund. I could not understand why she seemed so persistent, as she normally was very friendly with the rabbits, squirrels and chipmunks. I had to find out the cause of her excitement. The ravine was long, steep and slippery. After hitchhiking from one tree to another, I finally arrived at the bottom of the gully.

There stood Veslemor beside a raccoon. He was not a big fellow. I was surprised that Veslemor had attacked him, but there were many tracks and some blood in the white snow to indicate that there had been a royal fight. The mystery was solved, however, when I studied carefully the tracks in the snow: Two foxes had attempted to kill the raccoon. Apparently Veslemor had heard the commotion and had chased the foxes away.

I walked slowly toward the raccoon, which promptly prepared to defend himself. I noted his broad chest and his forelegs spread wide apart like those of a bulldog. He made short leaps toward me and a hissing sound came between his teeth like cold water hitting a hot frying pan. For his size, he looked formidable. When I talked to him in a low friendly voice, he moved closer but still maintained his guard. Then, after he approached near enough to obtain my scent, his belligerent attitude changed. He seemed glad to see me and with a whimpering, sorrowful cry, he lifted a front paw in a shake-hands gesture. Tired and haggard, he looked at me again, his dark eyes tormented; and he still held up his paw.

It was then that I recognized him, Todde the freeloader, an old friend of mine. I recalled the day in early spring when I first saw him sitting in the big oak watching me feed three young elghunds. After the dogs were through eating, he followed a long branch of the tree to the flat-roofed doghouse and thence to the ground, where he proceeded to clean up the dog food left in the pans. Thereafter, he had his own chow served on top of the doghouse. Although bread was his favorite menu, he also liked corn and apples. His home was in a hollow tree part way down the hill and the hole in the tree was just big enough to accommodate him. It was not long until the dogs became accustomed to him and the children of the neighborhood were attracted to their new pet.

When summer ended, cold weather set in and the dogs were moved to winter quarters, and Todde's food pan stood untouched on the flat-roofed doghouse and there were no raccoon tracks in the snow. I concluded that he had stored enough food for the winter and that he would show up in the spring like a hungry bear.

And now, here he was, skinny and raggedly tousled—hard to recognize. I wanted to ask him where he had been and why he had wandered away. Again he lifted his front paw with a sad cry, trying to tell me something. I started to walk, urging him to come home with me. Sure enough, he followed me to the foot of the hill, where he suddenly stopped and went into a convulsion. His head was bent down and his whole body quivered. I felt that this would be the last of him, but he recovered somewhat and turned back toward the ravine. As Todde seemed to be badly hurt I decided to take him to a veterinarian, but on Christmas Eve all offices would be closed. One thing that I could not understand was why Todde did not climb a tree when the foxes were trying to kill him.

With night fast approaching, I put Todde in a cardboard carton and left Veslemor to stand guard against the foxes. Both comrades of the previous summer went through the night without mishap.

Christmas morning broke bright and clear. The Bloomington animal warden brought a crate to transport the raccoon to the Cutlers veterinary hospital. It was nice and warm in the waiting room. When Dr. Bill opened the cover of the crate, Todde looked at him so trustingly. After an anaesthesia when the little fellow was lifted limply from the crate, two pieces of ice dropped from his front legs which had been frozen solid. Then I understood what he had been trying to tell me all along and then I knew why he had not climbed trees.

What suffering he had to endure! Held in a steel trap for days, only after his legs were frozen could he free himself from this gruesome invention.

The hollow oak still stands—his home—but it is empty now. Often I glance at the big branch over the flat-roofed doghouse, but Todde is not there. To save him, it would have been necessary to amputate both his front legs. A life without them would not have been a happy one for Todde.

CANVASBACKS AT LAKE CHRISTINA
Maytag Collection

A Letter to the President of the United States

Dear Mr. President:

Some time in the future, Mr. President, we hope that you will visit some of our national parks in America. It will be a wonderful experience, an adventure you will long remember. You would see the gleaming blue lakes, the shimmering streams, the sleepy lagoons, the waterfalls so high and mighty, thundering out between high and lofty mountains and mile after mile of virgin forests, deep, green and luscious. It is a rich and beautiful land.

But you will also notice the dead, empty wilderness outside the parks. You will see a few game birds but seldom a big game animal. Where once it was so rich with many game animals, that is now a thing of the past. It is as though a cold, clammy hand has suppressed all life in our fields and forests, and all that remains is a lifeless landscape and a lonely wilderness. We have millions of acres of field and forest, so overwhelmingly big and beautiful, but so empty and forsaken. We have begun to try to restock our wilderness, but with little success. In some places we have made a little advance but in most of the states the supply is dwindling fast. Most of our citizens picture our national parks as a reservoir for our wildlife, a place where our wildlife can live and breed in peace without being hunted or killed, and if some species become overstocked, the overflow can be moved, so we think, to other state parks, and from there into the wilderness. This, of course, has not been the case. The policy of the high and mighty in wildlife management has not been to remove or to plant any wild big game. Also since 1892 a few thousand animals have been removed; but that, of course, is just a drop in the bucket.

The removal and relocation of wild animals has been in operation for years, in many places on this earth. It is nothing new. Sweden started many years ago to trap moose and other animals where the food supply was not sufficient, and then move the animals and birds to better locations where there was more food. And this certainly has paid off. No country has done so much for their wildlife as the Swedes have done. They are the leaders today.

The authorities in the United States say that it is too expensive to replenish big game, that it costs between fifty and a hundred dollars per animal. However, the reports from other countries indicate that this estimate is too high. But let us face the larger truth: it is not an expense but a wonderful investment for the next generation, and some day, some time, they will be very grateful for our foresight.

A few years ago, Norway transported 300 reindeer to Greenland for replanting. The island never had any meat-producing herd before but now they have a healthy herd of 4,000 to 5,000. Newfoundland, which is not good moose country, received two moose, a bull and a cow in 1878. In 1904 four more moose were added to the herd. Today, Newfoundland, the island right at our back door, has a grand moose herd of 50,000.

From Southern Rhodesia comes the wonderful news that they now have removed and transplanted 6,000 animals, ranging from a foot-long snake to a six-ton elephant, from the rising water of Lake Kariba as the Zambesi River backs up against the huge dam in Kariba Gorge. But of course this is Africa not America.

We must not forget John Walsh and his heroic struggle against the rising water of the Surinam River in South America when the 218-foot-high Afobaka Dam was built and flooded the 4,700 square miles of Surinam's tropical rain forest. Here John Walsh and his gallant crew removed close to 10,000 animals and birds from the flooded jungle, a most impossible accomplishment. But where there is a will there is a way. In comparison, some of the citizens of Minnesota could not even remove and transplant 400 deer in the Twin Cities Arsenal grounds. The game warden was sent in to shoot the deer.

And now, Mr. President, let me be specific about the unwise procedures on Isle Royale.

Isle Royale! In the morning, haze rises out of crystal clear, blue-green water like a diamond in a sparkling setting, an island so peaceful, so inviting to tired mankind for a picnic or a restful vacation. Little do the happy visitors realize the brutal, gruesome, life-and-death struggle that occurs daily on this island. When the saga of our wildlife is written, the Isle Royale tragedy will stand out as the darkest, most shockingly horrid chapter in modern times.

I am going to tell you what has happened on Isle Royale in Lake Superior, something that is typical of unwise procedures in many areas. In those tragic years when fire was sweeping the island, when most of the moose population of Isle Royale died of starvation, as far as I know no animals were ever rescued from a terrible death. Now, of course, it is a different story. We have there thirty to forty wolves killing hundreds of young and full-grown moose. In its report the high and mighty claim that the wolf and moose population have struck a happy medium, that there is no increase in the moose herd. What is actually happening is that the wolves are killing off the moose. But who is killing off the wolves? What a magnificent conclusion! If Isle Royale had belonged to any other country, the leaders in that land would have started many years ago to remove some of the full-grown moose, and most of the young ones of eighteen months and over, and with some luck we would now have a mighty moose herd of several thousands in Minnesota, Wisconsin and Michigan.

There have been some articles in magazines and newspapers in later years that demonstrate so very well our lack of knowledge, understanding and care for our wildlife which is unparalleled any place in the civilized world. In many lands where the progress of the preservation of the wilderness and its inhabitants is far advanced, they have many large clubs and organizations which support this wonderful program in so many ways, but the *real* guardian is the government. As leaders in the work they have the best men they can obtain. These leaders have spent most of their lives in the forest. They know the life and habits of the wilderness. For these men the experimental stage has long since passed. Now, for them, the main thing is to save and protect what is left.

As far as some of the reports are concerned, they are very confusing articles. It is a pity that these scientists insist on trying to prove to the world that the healthiest thing for the moose population on the island is to have something like forty hungry wolves tear to pieces the old and sick ones. Those poor animals are supposed to be sacrificed in the interest of this project, and furthermore, the wolf does not kill only the old and sick ones. The fact is that often they slaughter for the lust to kill.

Now among true sportsmen in the world there is an unwritten law that says: "When you kill, kill fast and clean without causing unnecessary suffering." I am sure that this law has no meaning on Isle Royale. According to a report, they have 600 moose on the island; but there is no count of how many calves, yearlings or cows. In any report, these facts are very important. If there are only a few young ones, that means that the wolves have killed most of the calves. Or suppose that only ten or twenty percent of the cows are left—what future would the moose have?

The report also mentioned that there were between 30 and 40 wolves on the island but they were not actually sure of the number, However, they estimated that one moose is killed every three or four days by the wolves. In any man's language, this is a tremendous waste of our precious wild game. It means that in a year's time over 100 moose are killed. That, of course, does not include calves or young ones. Throughout the civilized world this shocking report travels, to those millions of friends of wilderness inhabitants. If those scientists would have taken time to study the history of most of the northern European countries, this experiment would not have been necessary. The moose have not changed in a hundred years; neither have the wolves changed their habits. In the history of Norway, the years between 1845 and 1855 were called the Wolf Years. Before that time the woods of Norway and Sweden were overstocked with wild game. In fact, half of the people in those countries lived by hunting and fishing.

Then the wolves came swarming in from Siberia into the northern parts of Norway—long, lanky, bony and hungry. At first they killed reindeer, and what they did not kill they scared into stampeding over the mountainsides. Then the wolves swung south and killed everything in their way. Some cattle were killed right in the stables and even fifteen horses in one district, and many outlying valleys were entirely vacated. People dared not go outside for days because of the hungry wolves outside the farm homes. How many people were killed by the wolves was never learned, but there were several.

By 1855 the wolves had reached the southern part of Norway. With the ocean in front of them, there was nothing to hunt, and back in the country there was nothing left of the wild game. Nothing was left there that could crawl or fly. Of the moose, sixteen were left in Hedemarken where the farmers were standing guard, and eight moose in Osterdalen. For the wolves there was nothing to hunt or run down. Then they started to kill each other and finally destroyed themselves.

If this contest on Isle Royale had been an experiment between the wolves and wolverines, then it would be an interesting experiment as they are both deadly killers. But here we have the moose which, when left alone, never kills anything; in fact, the moose is not even a meat-eater. On the other hand most hunters will place the wolves not far behind the wolverines in savage killing.

In a report it mentions the "kill" very lightly. They never explain how a 100-pound wolf can kill the biggest, the most powerful animal in our woods. Maybe it would be a good idea to describe how a pack of wolves can destroy this giant animal sometimes weighing close to 1,400 pounds and standing seven feet high.

The only way the wolves can kill a moose of that size is to run him down. If, for instance, two of these big moose start a fight and one strikes a blow at the opponent's shoulder with those knife-sharp hooves, it makes a cut that starts bleeding. As far as the wolves are concerned, the moose is dead because the wolves can smell blood a long distance, and the hunt is on. The pack never gives the moose a chance to rest, to sleep or eat. We must remember that wolves hunt in packs and also in relays. From three to five wolves will follow and fight the moose for hours, day after day, never giving him a chance to stop or lie down. When the first wolf pack gets tired, the second takes over to harass the moose.

If the hunt were out in the endless field and forest, the moose, able to run so much faster and longer, could get out of reach of the wolves. But on Isle Royale it is a different story. The moose has phenomenal hearing but very poor eyesight. He does not know that over the fifteen miles of water or ice there is another large country, the mainland, because he cannot see that far.

And so after three or four days with no sleep or food, he can hardly keep going. He tries to lie down but as soon as that happens, the wolves tear at him. So he staggers away again, only to sink down. He is ready for the big kill.

* * *

DRAMA NO. I

Then over the island rings a blood-chilling call from the wolves—"Come and get it!"—and from the different parts of the island come the answers of the hungry killers. If the moose has sunk down in deep snow and lies on his stomach, the wolves will leap on top of the moose.

Hungry animals with sharp teeth will slink in and rip out and tear the hide to shreds. More and more wolves swarm in. The poor animal will try to get up and shake those devils off, but his strength is gone. He opens his mouth and out into the frosty air goes a muffled scream of pain and torment and torture. Soon the shoulder blades and backbone are sticking out and the rib bones are laid bare. Some of the wolves are working at tearing out the hind parts. How long will the moose stay alive before death will free him? It might take a long time. For the poor animal, Dante's Inferno exists on Isle Royale. If the moose lies on his side, then the wolves will tear open his stomach and pull out his insides. If they can pull out the heart and lungs, then the torture will not last long. You may have read stories by some self-styled moose experts who claim they have seen wolves leap at a moose and in a single motion, slice the jugular vein and so the moose soon bleeds to death. That, of course, is a fantastic statement. A man who knows what he is talking about will tell you it takes a sharp knife and a strong arm to cut the short and tremendously thick and powerful bull neck.

* * *

DRAMA NO. II

The calving season for the moose is from the middle of April to some time in May, during which time one or two calves will be produced. As a rule when the cow is calving, she hunts a quiet place in peaceful surroundings. However, if the snow is deep and the snow-crust is thick and strong over the windswept island, the cow will find it very difficult to reach her calving place. The snow-crust will not carry the big animal and she will sink through and must rise up and press the crust down, which is very slow and tiresome labor. Here is another chance for the wolves to make a horrible kill. The wolves can travel swiftly and easily on top of the snow-crust. The cow cannot defend herself against fifteen to twenty wolves, and so another drama unfolds, so horrible that very few people can grasp it. Not only have we lost a cow, but also her offspring.

DRAMA NO. III

If the cow has been lucky enough to calve in peace, she is still not out of danger. The wolves can smell the newborn calf and the cow's afterbirth for a long distance. They soon have the cow located and a fight progresses. The small, young calf on his wobbly long legs will try to stand as close to his mother as possible, but the mother must fight off fifteen wolves and strike with her front hooves. Often a dark shadow sneaks between the calf and his mother; the wolves knock over the calf and sink their teeth into the throat and rip it open. When the mother turns around and looks after her offspring, the calf is dead and the wolves are gone.

As for the old and sick ones, it certainly is an inhuman act to willfully sacrifice the poor animal, allowing it to be ripped, pulled and chewed to pieces, to die a thousand deaths. In a report, it tells of a cow—shown in a picture—facing a whole pack of wolves. In many places the snow is blood-soaked after a terrible and hopeless struggle. This moose cow leaped to her death over a mountain cliff rather than be chewed to pieces. Millions of our citizens, so proud of our great land, would bow their heads in shame over this man-created Isle Royale tragedy, and I hope that the Humane Society of the United States will stop this unbelievable, gruesome slaughter of our king of the forest.

And now, Mr. President, let us look at the economic aspect of it.

If there were a gold mine on this Isle Royale and robbers were stealing our gold, we would send a whole army to capture them, but for our wildlife, nobody lifts a finger in this life-and-death struggle, and the outcome is never in doubt. If this foolish and dreadful tragedy occurred in any other country, an array of faithful wilderness friends by the thousands would stage a march on their government and demand an immediate stop to this gruesome experiment.

Minnesota is a great tourist state where the tourist leaves behind approximately 300 to 500 million dollars a year. They like to fish and they admire our beautiful lakes; but ask the tourist who travels into Canada what his biggest thrill was on the trip and he will always say it was the never-to-be-forgotten sight of the caribou, the elk or bear or the big bull moose standing with his great lofty crown looking over his kingdom.

Isle Royale as a wild animal park could be one of our greatest attractions, something much more precious than gold, silver or jewels. If our government could see the possibilities and appropriate the money, or if some private citizens would donate the money as a memorial, it could be the most precious attraction we have.

What should we do? We should as soon as possible separate the wolves from the moose. The King of the Forest has certainly suffered enough. The next step would be to start a study course, enrolling students from the age of eighteen and up. We could also seek help from other countries, those who are much more advanced in these projects than we are. We in Minnesota have excellent facilities for a wildlife college. We have the Fort Snelling area, an old military fort with many buildings standing empty. Here we could start the program with teachers who have studied the wilderness and our fauna, men who are rich in knowledge from many years of service. Our game wardens could be used as first-rate teachers.

We would in a short time have a wonderful herd of healthy moose. The young elk yearlings would be shipped from other states and from Canada, and also caribou and bears and many other specimens as well as animals and birds from foreign countries. After a few years of healthy living, the caribou, elk and moose yearlings which have lived in peace for a year could be rounded up and shipped to other places that have enough food, water and space available. This would be the very first project of this kind in the United States. In time, maybe we would have ten to twenty localities in different states, including Alaska. The students graduating from the Wild Game Course would hopefully teach others. This would be a great step in the right direction—a tremendous help for the progress and preservation of our heritage.

It would be a good idea to let the citizens of the country know how much it actually costs to feed the wolves in a year's time. Let us compare Isle Royale with some of the projects in the Scandinavian countries: for instance, the Mathisen Esvold Verks in Norway. This is a vast wilderness, privately owned by a company for lumbering and pulpwood.

The leaders in the project have in the last ten years kept a strict control over the harvest of moose in this territory. We find that the average slaughter-weight of the moose is about 400 pounds. Slaughter-weight is the weight of edible meat taken from a moose, excluding the rest of the carcass. We know that the Isle Royale moose is much bigger, the average slaughter-weight would be at least 500 pounds. According to some reports, a moose is killed every three or four days. That means 125 moose a year. If we set the price on moose meat at 75 cents a pound, then the feeding bill for the wolf population would be over $50,000 a year. That does not include all the yearlings and calves. In years it would run to millions of dollars.

In this country we have thousands of poor and hungry people who live mostly on greasy hamburger and bread—because they cannot afford any better food. It seems incredible that we let the wolves consume hundreds of tons of excellent moose meat when we have so many hungry people walking the streets. It has happened in some foreign lands that we are called ugly ducklings. I do resent the title. The American people are just as handsome as people in any nation on this earth, but I will bow my head in shame in view of the Isle Royale gruesome tragedy, because in that enterprise we are at the borderline of insanity.

Many will not understand the modern way to hunt and check the moose herd, count the old and the sick ones, and also mark the young ones. There are many ways this can be done. One way is the use of the Norwegian elghund. This is the same breed of dog that they use in Norway and Sweden when they harvest over 45,000 moose a year. Also in Sweden they have an excelent hunting dog, the jamthund. The Norwegian elghund is an outstanding hunting dog. He is well trained, well bred and expensive, and often worth his weight in gold. Please do not confuse these hunting dogs with the $35 to $45 elkhound puppies you can pick up in this country. Nobody can raise a healthy, first-rate puppy for less than seventy-five to a hundred dollars.

On the hunting trail, the hunter will select the terrain and start walking in a fairly straight line, always against the wind. The elghund will cover both sides of the path or line, always crossing and recrossing the path. He might travel a half mile out from both sides. When he finds a moose track, he figures out which direction the moose has gone, and also how old the tracks are, and how fast the moose has traveled. If he has traveled at a rapid speed he would be in another valley in a short time. The elghund does not rely entirely on the tracks as does the beagle or basset. You will often find him standing on his hind legs so as to take the scents in the air. He knows that the air currents do not always follow the contour of the land. He will often be able to take a scent for the distance of a mile or two and then go directly to where the moose stands.

If the elghund disappears for any length of time, the hunter must start listening for the dog's voice which means that he might have a moose. The way the elghund approaches the moose is very important. If it is a cow with a calf, he must ignore them except in counting. If it is a young bull, he must approach the young one with utmost care and not scare him into headlong flight. The dog takes his time. There might be some trees that need watering or some grass that must be smelled, but he is always creeping up on the bull. If the bull does not look too scared, then the dog moves in and tries a muffled "Woof." If nothing happens, the next woof will be louder and soon his voice comes clear and loud so that the hunter can easily find where the stand is. If the moose is a big bull and a tough guy, the elghund moves in more directly and often picks a fight with the big fellow. The moose gets mad at the dog and tries to strike him with his front hooves, but the elghund must bounce out of the way. Often the moose is so mad at the little intruder that he will not notice the hunter only ten steps away.

The same procedure will occur when the moose herd is checked and counted. The hunter will mark the cow with the calf, and also the yearlings. As for the older bulls, it is easy to observe in the short distance if a bull is in good health or if he is old and sick. There are many other ways to keep track of the moose herds and its members.

In addition to thoroughly checking the moose herd on Isle Royale, the wolves should be moved to one of the many other islands in Lake Superior. The wolves would still have their freedom. We must realize that the wolves have many friends and provide an interesting study. In those instances where the moose is sick or too old, he could be shot (the bullet not less than 9 mm.) and fed to the wolves. So many things can be done, but the time is short.

From Washington comes the report that we are now spending too much money on our farm program and the farm schools. It might be because of the way the big ones gobbled up the small family farms. (They certainly disappeared in a hurry.) So why don't we promote this wonderful project and get our bright young men, with hearts and souls in the right place, to study and learn and help care for our precious wilderness? Here is a phase where we do not need a subsidy for overprotection, or for politics, or for the cold or the hot war. This would be a project for the future of America.

Norway and Sweden have a yearly harvest of 45,000 moose. If they harvest one of every four, that means those countries have a moose herd of over 140,000. And compare the space in these small countries with our millions and millions of acres of wilderness. Those countries have learned to take care of the wilderness, and learned it the hard way. For those leaders the experimental stage has long since passed. Now, for them, the important thing is to save and protect what is left for the coming generation. There is one thing certain in those countries: no packs of hungry wolves are ever allowed to tear to pieces His Royal Highness, the King of the Forest Himself. He is a national asset to any land.

Through the last thirty years we have had many great presidents. We had President Roosevelt and his New Deal, Harry Truman and his Square Deal, and John Kennedy and the New Frontier. But throughout these three decades the wilderness and its inhabitants have not had a new deal or a square deal. We hope the New Day will arrive for the wildlife as well as for the people.

We are at a crossroads now. We need the help and support of all if our rich country is not to become lonesome, desolate, empty of life and beautiful wild creatures.

* * *

Have you dreamed about the moonlight on the silvery water?
Have you seen a million stars twinkle on a winter night?
Or hiked the hills on skis through the white, silent wonderland?
Or listened to a bubbling brook in spring?
Have you wandered through the woods on an autumn day,
Lazy-like with plenty of time?
Hunted for the sport of hunting—not with the lust to kill?

The Timber Wolf

No wild animals were more hated and feared than the big timber wolf in those countries where he was free to roam, hunt and kill. That is the way it has been for thousands of years and will be in the future. In the olden days a pack of hungry wolves would come swarming into a small valley where people did not have modern weapons to defend themselves, at a time when the rifle was very slow and a cumbersome hunting weapon and it often misfired so that in many cases it was the end of the man behind the gun. Some cold winter nights when the wolves sent out those bone-chilling howls, people's blood froze in their veins as they stood helplessly watching their precious farm animals being torn to pieces. Farm after farm was stripped of animals; even full-grown horses were killed right in the barn. Those were hard times, often worse than war.

In northern parts of Norway and Sweden, the wolves often came in from Siberia to attack the reindeer. The Lapps, who own the reindeer herds, stand guard day and night. Even so, many a reindeer is killed in winter. Often it is not for food but just for the pleasure of the kill. In our day in that part of Norway, the wolves were hunted down with airplanes.

The last wolf was killed in Denmark in 1813, in England in 1500, in Scotland in 1743 and in Ireland in 1770. In the United States there is not a single animal that would stand a chance for his life if he had to fight off a pack of hungry wolves.

The wolf has lots of courage when he is in a pack, but singly he is cowardly and sneaky and often kills for the lust of killing. He does not have the dog's open, faithful, trusting eyes. His eyes are yellow and slanted. He is out of place in the world of today. Because of his size and tremendous appetite, he cannot find enough food to satisfy his hunger. A full-grown wolf will consume from 8 to 14 pounds of meat in twenty-four hours. Some years ago there were lots of wolves in the Northwest and they had a good living at the time. Seldom did a wolf kill any domesticated animal. He sometimes picked up a chicken or two, but the fields and woods were rich with prey, small wild animals and birds, and oftentimes if a farm horse or cow or pig died, it was hauled out in the grove or ravine where the wild animals had a feast. Also, in those days, the farmer killed the newborn calves because beef was cheap and there was no sale for calf meat. Since he could sell the milk, the calf was killed and thrown out to the wild animals.

Times have changed. If an animal dies now the fertilizer plant will pick up the dead animal, move it to the plant and convert it to fertilizer. The price of meat has skyrocketed so that no farmer ever kills a calf or throws it in the field. On the farm and in the forest there were lots of raccoons, woodchucks, and gophers in those days. That is also a thing of the past. Raccoons and woodchucks are seldom seen, and if the farmer has gophers in his field now, he pours poison into the hole. Field after field is free of gophers.

For the wolves it is now a dark day. To satisfy his ravenous hunger he has to attack farm animals such as sheep, pigs, calves and chickens. If he cannot find enough small wild animals, he has to tackle the big game such as deer, bear, moose and elk, which means a prolonged, dreadful, life-and-death struggle for these large creatures.

It is against Nature's own law. The rule of the wild is that a predator is much stronger and bigger than the prey and the killing is fast and without delay. When a wolf kills a fox, it is done in a few seconds; when a fox kills a rabbit, we hear a muffled scream and it is all over. When a hawk swoops down on a bird, he jabs his beak in between the bird's shoulder blades a couple of times and the bird is dead. But if the predator has to tackle the big animals, then it will be a long, gruesome fight in which the big and strong will be torn to pieces, piece by piece, limb by limb, by the packs.

Many people will ask what wolves are good for. I can honestly answer that I do not know. The wolf is living in a lost world where his task as an important link in the wilderness cycle is no more. Singly, he is not any worse than coyotes or lynx when he kills for food to satisfy his hunger. However, in packs, he is insatiably bloodthirsty and shows no mercy. One thing is certain: in those countries where he is no more, the people will say: "Thank God we do not have to fear or listen to those bloodcurdling howls any more."

Not so long ago Minnesota had a wonderful herd of over 650,000 deer roaming in the woods and fields and it was really something to see and brag about. Too bad it could not last. Now the deer are disappearing at a very fast rate, just like all other wild game and birds that used to roam all over the state. In fact, inside a few years, they will all be dead and gone.

Minnesota also has a small breeding stock of moose wandering up in the north woods. In 1922, the moose hunting season was closed and it was estimated that the moose population at that time was 2,000 head, more or less. In the following years, these animals were seldom seen and noticed and the hunting season on the moose was closed. In 1964, it was estimated that the herd had reached the 4,500 mark and the Game Department would like a limited open season on the now big moose herd, but it was rejected. In 1969, the Game Department asked again for an open hunting season on the now fabulous moose herd of 8,000. They claimed that some of the animals would starve to death and the only way to prevent it was to harvest some of the moose. It seems incredible that a moose herd of 2,000 in 1922 could only produce 2,500 offspring in 42 years (from 1922 to 1964) and then in the next three years, increase the moose population by 3,500 (from 4,500 to 8,000). The fact is that when the deer are killed off, the moose will be the next species to be destroyed and it should not take too long with 400 wolves divided up into many packs, howling and killing all over the woods and wilderness. The young moose will be the first to be killed and then the breeding stock. When the deer and moose are killed off, what are the wolves supposed to live off? The defenders of our wildlife must now decide which is more important for our American heritage, either the deer, moose or wolves. There is no middle-of-the-road decision to make. Either they must take a stand to harvest some of the tremendous wolf population or decide that the marauder is more important to our environment than the deer and moose.

Nobody will have much success raising vegetables in his garden if a herd of goats is trampling and roaming all over, and it is the same way with the big game and the wolves. In the long run they will be too numerous and the prey too few. It has been tried in many foreign countries but with the same discouraging result. Only after the wolf was eliminated did the game come back. So long as the wolves have plenty of wild game to kill and the citizens think it is a wonderful thing to have those marauders slaughter the wildlife, there is not much we can do about it. But when the time comes when there is no more big game for the wolves to kill, and when hunger and starvation are tearing at his intestines, then it will be a different story. Then are the leaders in conservation ready and able to defend the farmer and his cattle in our north woods against the starving wolf packs or will it be the same horrible situation that existed in so many of Europe's countries some centuries ago? There is no difference between the Siberian wolf and our big timber wolves; only the amount of food in his stomach makes the difference.

I am not in favor of killing all the wolves, but we do have too many, and to have all that beautiful game destroyed is a tragedy and an incredible loss to our country and future generations.

In Norway they have only ten wolf families, each living in a different valley and so far apart that there is no chance of them gathering in packs. So far it has worked out very well. The folks there seldom see or notice the wolves, although a few of the domestic animals are killed. Of course, the Game Department controls the size of the wolf families so that the wolves cannot either become too numerous or starve to death. They will find plenty of small prey to live on.

It might also be the answer to the welfare of the wolf population in Minnesota and it certainly would be worth trying before all his prey in the woods are gone. Then wolf packs will start killing farm animals on a big scale and nobody will be safe. If and when that happens, they will be hunted down to the last one, and we do not want that to happen.

Some years ago the city of Shakopee, Minnesota, had a wolf family living in the woods down by the river and I don't think there were many people in that city who knew about the uninvited guests. In fact, as far as I know no farm animals were ever reported killed by the wolf family. They lived off the land.

But as long as the wolves can form packs, they will turn into deadly killers, and that also holds true sometimes with dogs. Ordinary dogs and hunting dogs become killers of game. Yes, even human beings lose all common sense and form riot mobs that burn, loot and kill.

For a century the Conservation Department has followed the old course of trying to sell as many hunting licenses as possible, and let the wild animals and birds take a terrible beating. We are now at the end of the line and there will be very little hunting for years to come. We must change our ways and methods. If overcrowded and starving wild animals become a problem, we must move them out by helicopter, by trucks and other vehicles to places where they have more room and better living conditions. And I hope that the two or three hundred thousand hunters who have for years hunted our fauna will now cease this practice. I hope they will put their shoulders to the wheel and help in a big way to replant and restore our fauna. If not, we will soon become a very poor wild game land.

To merely replant some fish in a few lakes in the future will not be enough. We are racing against time. Only the future will tell. And to harvest some of the wolves should be a job for the game wardens and the very best sharpshooters. Under no circumstances should the wolves be trapped or hunted down by amateurs.

In books and magazines in recent years there have been many delightful stories about people who have found and raised a litter of wolf puppies. Many sled teams in America have half-breeds, a cross between a wolf and a dog. They are strong and fast and excellent sled-dogs. Yes, if people have intelligence and patience, they can make a pet out of most of our wildlife. In many places we find young moose, deer, bear and many other wild animals as pets, often tenderly loved members of the household. Many of them are free to come and go and they consider human beings as their special friends and benefactors.

A Gruesome Sight

One stormy morning on Lake Superior two fishermen in a small boat searched and found a landing place on Isle Royale where they could pull the boat upon shore and wait for the storm to subside. While waiting they decided to explore the island, and in doing so came upon some wolf tracks in the snow. They followed the tracks and soon more tracks appeared. They reached a battlefield where a fight had occurred between a moose and a big pack of wolves. Hermann Baxle wrote the following description of the battle:

"I have in my long life seen and heard of many cruel episodes in the wilderness, but this was the most gruesome I have ever seen. It was very easy to see what had happened. It seems that the moose had been walking up a small hill and over the ridge he had stumbled and fallen over on his side, with the wolves in hard pursuit. Undoubtedly this animal had been chased and harried for days and nights without rest or food. Here, the whole pack had attacked him, ripped and torn the hide to pieces. Even chunks of meat were left on pieces of the hide and there was blood all over.

"Then it would appear that the moose had actually gotten to his feet, staggered, and was trying to run. At the start of our trail we could not figure out what had happened, but farther on we found parts of the moose—guts that he had stepped on. Then we understood that his stomach had been ripped open and that he had dragged the guts after him. He had tried to walk sideways a couple of times so as not to step on his guts. By this time, my son John had seen enough; he started to vomit and could not stand it any longer. So I told him to return to the boat. This he gladly did. I followed the bloody trail about two hundred yards. All the way I could see how the wolves had hung on and the poor animal had dragged them along. The moose had tried to reach a place in the woods where the trees were thick and where he would have a better chance to fight off these devils. But he did not make it.

"It was easy to locate the place where the wolves had conquered. It was by far the most appalling mass of horror I have ever seen. The snow in a wide circle was soaked with blood, where bones and parts of hairy chunks were strewn all over. Part of the moose was still there—ripped and torn head and limbs.

"In the afternoon the storm died down and we reached home in good time. But the horrible sight of the moose's slaughter bothered us both through the night. The next morning, I described our experience to some other fishermen and three of them decided to see this gruesome tragedy for themselves.

"I read your comments in the Minneapolis newspapers, and I most earnestly agree with you. It is a shocking, horrid chapter in our wildlife management."

Wolves' Heaven

His name is George. He is the Supreme Commander of all the Wolf Nobility on Isle Royale, the Wolf's Kingdom, the Wolf's Heaven on this earth.

When an emergency arises on this island, concerning the wolf population, the Supreme Commander lets it be known that a meeting of the Wolf Nobility will be held in the Devil's Dance Hall, and he wants all the wolves to be present. Nobody will be excused.

At a meeting in March 1963, the Supreme Commander was informed by his private secretary that an article in a magazine for February had some insulting information concerning the Wolf Nobility on Isle Royale. In this article, the Men of Higher Learning claimed that the Wolf Nobility had very poor table manners. In fact, the article stated that the wolves do not eat their food, but gulp it down, and furthermore, they gorge themselves to the extent that they can hardly walk. The worst part of it is that the Men of Higher Knowledge claim that the wolves don't leave anything on their plates after the meal, not even some pieces of meat. The men insist that the wolves consume the whole moose, even head and hair. When they are through there is nothing left, not even enough bones to make a good study of the moose herd's health.

The majority of the wolves are very disturbed about these statements in the magazine, but George, the Supreme Commander, proclaims that these great men of superior knowledge are their friends and protectors. "Those men have spent from three to five years glorifying our nobility. In fact, we are the leaders of the wolf population in the world, an example for the rest of the wild animals. I would not be surprised if my name in the future would be St. George. What we need now is some excellent teamwork between ourselves and the great men.

"We are the United States Government's guests on this island and the government is very concerned about our health and welfare. You must know that the government has sent those Men of Higher Learning to check our health and well-being. Of course, they are very much concerned about the food that we consume in this wolf's paradise. In no place on earth has our race had the fortune to be so highly honored, so handsomely glorified as we are today. Now I want all of you to give those fellows, those wonderful men, the scientists, our full cooperation. From now on we will slaughter the moose, but not eat the body, just leave the carcass until the day or the day after, so that our friends, the scientists, will have a chance to inspect the carcass. I am not sure what the men are looking for, but maybe they want to find out if the moose wash their ears, brush their teeth or see the dentist twice a year. Whatever they are looking for, it must be very important for our health and welfare. We have to remember that millions of two-legged, pale-faced people have for years and years had only sloppy, greasy hamburger and bread to eat, and nothing else has been their main food. We have had some wonderful moose meat. Those things are only for our nobility to enjoy. There also is another inportant fact that we must not forget. When we organize to run down, slaughter and rip to pieces a big moose, don't forget to howl, long, loud and clear, because those wonderful fellows, those Ph.D.'s, love to hear the howl. It is such a thrill, so sensational, so divine to listen to. In fact, these men of higher learning call that wonderful music. So don't forget, make it long and loud."

Well, it might sound like music to those city-born gentlemen, but not to the moose.

It seems that George, the supreme commander, was an outstanding leader and a great public relations man—because now the wolf leaves the carcass for the scientists to inspect. Now, only after three months, those men have inspected more carcasses than in all the previous three to five years.

However, an emergency meeting in the Devil's Dance Hall was called. The whole Wolf Nobility was up in arms because of a magazine article printed sometime later, wherein the scientists stated that there was so much sickness in the moose population on Isle Royale that it was terrible. The wolves felt that it was incredible that the United States Government could not have inspected the moose population before. The Wolf Nobility was in a frenzy, madder than hell. They were outraged to think that they had consumed so many sick animals. It was no wonder that the wolves on Isle Royale did not drool anymore, they just spit out the moose meat. The moose meat from the Wolf's Heaven, Isle Royale, was not fit for wolf consumption, only for the human race.

Recently, a delegation from the Isle Royale Wolves' Nobility was on its way to Washington to demand that the moose meat, now and in the future, be flown in from Canada or Newfoundland or Alaska, and that under no circumstances would moose meat from Isle Royale be consumed by wolves. The meat was only good for human consumption. Furthermore, the moose meat from the foreign countries must bear the U.S.A. blue stamp of approval and be fit for wolf food.

Some time ago, a newspaperman asked George, as he was about to appear before the investigating committee, how many millions of dollars worth of moose meat the wolves on Isle Royale had consumed in recent years. George, without blinking an eye, answered that he would have to invoke the Fifth Amendment.

On Wildlife Management

There is an old saying that no organization is stronger than the men responsible for its functioning. The same holds true for the organization of the wildlife division. It is the men behind the programs that are responsible. The Secretary of the Interior is appointed by the President of the United States and it is also a political position. And as a rule his time in office is the length of time that the appointing political party is in the driver's seat. This, of course, is a big stumbling block, a big drawback for the welfare of our country and our fauna. The Secretary of the Interior should be selected by the U. S. Civil Service organization, and the best man for the job, regardless of parties, should be chosen. Furthermore, when he fills the position, in order to be sure of the best interests and welfare of our wildlife, the job should be his as long as his service was good and satisfactory.

Our wildlife management is and will be in time to come, a very important cog in the vast, beneficently running machinery of our national life and our country's welfare. But to change the commander-in-chief every so often is very bad for the department and all its functioning. It is not an easy task even for a good man to take over the department and start to give orders and change things when the governing body, the bureaucracy of the organization has been in power and control for so many years and are well settled in their ways and methods. I believe that it is just here that the focal point lies, the reason why this department has for years dragged its feet. "Too little and too late"—it is the old dire slogan. Agriculture and that department having to do with livestock have in the last ten to fifteen years made tremendous progress, often doubling the output. So why hasn't our wildlife management tried to follow in their footsteps? What we need now is some farsighted men that are willing and able to tackle new ideas and methods with an open mind.

There is also another rule and law in the wildlife department and that is that no game warden with only a high school education can ever hold a higher post—not *any* game warden, regardless of his ability and experience and knowledge (an unbelievable rule unparalleled in any other country in the world). I earnestly believe that it is from the rank and file of this great organization that we can select some very great leaders and trail blazers in all kinds of splendid new directions. A degree from a college or university does not make an expert in the field and forest. No, it is what the young man learns *after* graduation that counts. If he could spend some years in the field and forest in company with a good game warden, then and only then would he know the score.

In my own quite wide experience—as a member of wildlife organizations in many lands and as one who knows well many of our wise and humane game wardens in Minnesota and Canada, I think it is most regrettable that there is a ceiling over them and that they can advance no higher in their great potential usefulness to our country. And let me also say earnestly that high-degree university men who have only been sitting in offices are often lacking in vision and strength and can seriously hinder and not help a good and necessary program.

In my correspondence with the wildlife department, I find many glaring statements that are so contrary to facts that it is a pity. Here is a quotation from a letter that I received in regard to my report— and horrified objection — to the department's wolf and moose procedure on Isle Royale: "The predations by wolf on the moose is no more or less vicious or inhumane than the use of rodents by hawks and eagles, coyotes and badgers, etc." Blessed be ignorance! Here is a man who undoubtedly has a high position in a department but has never seen a fox or coyote catch a gopher and, in a split second, crush the rodent between powerful jaws with strong teeth. There are no coyotes or foxes which will carry or play nurse maid to a scratching, biting rodent. Their lips and mouths would, in a short time, be a bloody mess, so the killing is fast and without delay.

To compare a little episode like this, that only lasts a second, to a gruesome tragedy when a hungry pack of wolves slaughters, rips, pulls, chews a big moose to pieces bit by bit, limb by limb, with terrible suffering and pain, which must seem to the poor animal to last a lifetime, is sad. When, after a long time, he finally drags his last breath and his struggle is over, no human being who knows and understands the wilderness would ever compare these tragic events. If we have many of such men in the department, then to restock or replant our wilderness will be a long and cumbersome struggle.

Now if this most learned, highly educated office man would have called in a game warden and asked him to explain the difference in a killing method, he would not make a statement like that. Yes, in the wildlife department there are too many fellows who were born and reared in town and who never had any true contact with wild animals—no affectionate, fascinated observation of them, winter, spring and summer, in the sunlight and in the dark of the moon. For only with that comes the alert intelligence to understand the life struggles and rules of the wilderness, and most important of all, the feeling for our fauna.

Justice for All

On a bright sunny day in March we were on our way to inspect some beaver colonies outside a big town in central Sweden. There were three colonies built on a quiet, fast-flowing stream. The dikes formed a good-sized lake which in summer was a haven for ducks and geese. As we were standing there admiring the interesting project, two busloads of Sunday school children of all ages arrived with their teacher and the bus driver as a guide. The snow was deep but trails were made in various directions so that the children could see and admire the beavers' engineering skill and also their lumberjack way of doing things. The children followed the teachers with great interest as they explained the wonderful ways the beavers help to conserve the lakes and forests.

When Mr. and Mrs. Beaver crawled on top of their hut and sat there in the sun, the children's enthusiasm was unlimited. The last event of the tour was when the youngsters helped the bus driver toss into the stream some bundles of tree branches which floated down to the beaver dam. The driver explained that other young people had gathered the bundles of branches and had placed them along the stream to make sure that the beavers did not starve during the long, cold winter with its deep snow.

From my window in my home I can see a beaver colony and watch its fascinating life. Many a youngster comes to the beaver dam. The boys are well equipped with guns and bows and arrows. They sit waiting for a chance to kill. After the first hard frost with strong, thick ice forming on the lake, the beaver hut looks like a heap of scrap iron with all those steel traps set for the poor creatures.

Those young boys are not any worse or any better than the rest of the youngsters in our world. It is the lack of education and life guidelines that is missing. The schools, religious institutions and the churches have for 2000 years preached the sermon to worship and glorify the Creator, but have so far completely ignored or forgotten the Creation itself. The time has come for the leaders in all schools and spiritual institutions to include and promote the fundamental truths in life itself and develop respect for all living things in our environment.

If the human race is lucky enough to survive in the coming years there might still be time to correct many of this world's ills. The human race has for centuries proclaimed that we are the masters on this earth. We have been aggressive and greedy and often use brutal force to conquer our fellow travelers and have so completely ignored their place in the sun. It must be a new day for the next generation, a wider horizon and a better understanding of their environment to include all living things. They must have a chance to study nature's interesting creation, its mood, tone and colors and also have a chance to see, feel and listen to nature's manifold sounds. We need a nature study now; we need it badly. It is here that the Church could do a tremendous amount of good for the human race.

* * *

The meat locker plant was crowded when an overweight man waddled in and proudly dumped 24 wild ducks on the floor, his proud eyes wandering here and there over the gathering, triumphantly waiting for the murmurs of admiration for his great success. One of his offspring, a lanky boy of 12 or 13, related with lots of grimaces how his dad had shot all those ducks in a few minutes.

He had visited a farm just outside the city last summer where a boy and girl had collected Easter ducklings from people who could not keep the birds any longer—and all through the summer they had fed and taken care of these unwanted birds. Now when the duck season opened, the birds were big and fat and the boy had told his dad, and before daybreak they were at the farm. Of course, the farm was posted "No Hunting," but it did not take long to remove the sign.

"Then at sunrise my dad, with his gun, walked down to the feeding place in the lake. From a bucket he threw some corn out over the lake, in a small circle close to shore. He then called for the ducks to come and get it. They came from all directions, hungry and unafraid of people. Then my dad walked back from the lake and let them have it—five, six shots—Bang! Bang! And only two ducks got away, but they could not fly because they had been hurt and so they headed into some weeds. But my dad did not have more shells in his gun so he let them go."

There was a deathlike quiet in the locker plant. A sarcastic grin flashed over some of the faces, and one after another of the persons there walked out. Soon the bull frog with his offspring was left alone. The owner of the locker plant told this miserable human being to pick up the ducks and get out of the place. He said he did not want anything to do with either him or his ducks.

Outside, the father opened his trunk door and dumped the sack in the back of his car. Inside, his automobile was full of kids rolling all over, with some of them hanging out of the open car windows. To me it looked like a bird's nest full of young ones with outstretched necks and open mouths screaming for food.

I had to get out to the Torgesen's farm in a hurry. That was where he had slaughtered the ducks. Peter and Maggie must be very sad, crying their eyes out. When I drove into the farmyard it was quiet and peaceful. There was no sign of the tragedy, or this slaughtering of ducks in the morning. A neighbor told me that the Torgesens were visiting his brother and they had been gone for a couple of days, but they should be back any time now. This neighbor had witnessed the murderous ordeal in the morning and after the father had left, he had walked around the lake to be sure there were no cripples left. He had found one duck dead on the shore, but one more had taken off in flight and seemed not to be hurt too badly.

Soon the Torgesens drove in and before the car stopped, the youngsters were on their way to the lake. They were calling for their ducks, their pets. But there was no fluttering of wings, no happy squawk from any ducks.

Now this neighbor was the kind of man a neighbor should be. He called Peter and Maggie over and explained that the duck season had opened that very morning and rather than having somebody killing those beautiful jeweled mallards, he had taken his gun down to the lake shore and shot it in the air and scared the hell out of the ducks, and by now they all were on their flight to the south. Those youngsters looked very sad for a while. Then Maggie's face lit up into a bright smile.

"Wonderful!" she said. "Now they will be back next spring. Then they will be big enough to lay eggs and then we can raise ducklings."

I was looking at the neighbor. Boy, what a liar he was! Now I am wondering if a white lie is really a lie if it can do so much good.

* * *

The war was over and a good friend of mine in Norway asked if I would purchase a shotgun for him, because the Germans had confiscated his. I selected the best automatic gun with its 5-shell chamber and informed him that it would be delivered by a mutual friend. I immediately received a telegram from him, "Please send a single-shot, not the automatic."

Two years later, on my visit to his home, he explained that if he went hunting with that murderous automatic, he would be a disgrace among decent hunters. Their slogan is, "Give the game birds a chance."

* * *

There was an elegant party in a beautiful home. The food was excellent and well served. I was looking forward to the second course, wild grouse from the neighboring forest. This species had been nearly extinct some years before, but with careful game management, had been making a good comeback.

The charming host encouraged me to take a big helping, but a friend beside me whispered, "Take only a taste." The host was a big landowner and his forests were recognized for their rich game. However, on the platter there was only enough of this wonderful bird for a good taste for each person.

After dinner my friend explained that he didn't shoot this bird to get the limit, only to get the taste.

Deer Snaring in the North Woods

This story from a Minneapolis newspaper is a cruel and harrowing account of unsportsmanlike conduct in the north woods, specifically the snaring and strangulation of eight deer on the Trout Lake Portage at Lake Vermilion near Tower, Minnesota. It is a story told by a man who owns a cabin and some land on the portage.

"I received a call from a retired forest ranger at Tower. He said he was checking my property and found six deer strangled in wire snares near the cabin. He called the game warden and found two more deer strangled to death six miles west of the cabin where the deer had been yarded up for the winter. The snares had been set high in the trail, obviously in hopes of killing the deer and using them as wolf bait. The game warden arrested two men on deer snaring charges and they were fined $50 each by the justice of the peace."

I am sure that those men in the future will have great awe and respect for our justice of the peace and the law that protects our fauna when there is this dire penalty of only $12.50 per deer for stringing it up and letting it hang there on a wire until it is dead! Where is the justice in our north woods?

The time has come to overhaul some of our outmoded laws and shake out some of those moth-eaten law books. Soft talk and small fines are not the answer to the problem or the way to handle the wilderness. Gangsters with silk gloves will not improve this situation. Too many of these hoodlums have for years laughed at our judges and trampled on our laws and rules. They understand only one language—a big fine and a long jail sentence.

THE PRAIRIE CHICKEN — Roger Preuss — The Thomas D. Murphy Company

Farewell to the Prairie Chicken

My first visit to North Dakota was in the middle of November, 1922, when wet snow covered fields and meadows. To the horizon, as far as the eye could see, was mile after mile of prairie land, the richest fertile soil, unbelievably wide and seemingly endless! This was the world-famous Red River Valley, the breadbasket of the world.

Over the fields tumbleweeds rolled, bouncing, traveling with the wind. Only when a fence or some obstacle would block their progress would they stop for a resting place. The farms were big and wide in this Scandinavian settlement with some sheltering trees on the north side and with new modern houses most two stories high. The red barns loomed even bigger in all this vast whiteness. It was a rich land, a land of proud farmers. The white, spacious church with its slender tower stood like a monument to the folks' life and progress.

It was quiet and peaceful on the prairie in the wintertime, not much to see or do. To visit the next neighbor's farm, which was two miles away, was like a trip to town. The highlight was in the evening when we called the horses, twenty-eight of them in all, and they came toward the barn, trotting, galloping. They knew that hay and oats were waiting in their cribs.

Some winter nights the full moon would sail bright and clear over the snow-covered fields and meadows, which would paint the prairie in a fantastically beautiful, silver-colored landscape. Often rabbits, fox and coyotes would wander over the shining land.

Spring came creeping slow and bashfully, afraid to disturb the prairie's long, deep winter slumber. It started one morning with melting snow and the rush and noise in the downspouts. It was a welcome sight and sound. Later the snow started melting on the south side of the straw stacks, and over on the field some black dirt started peeking through on the high ridges. Out on the prairie some water potholes appeared like some mirrors over the flat land.

Some years before, I had visited a small valley in Norway with high mountains on three sides, where for two months in winter the sunbeams did not shine in the bottom of the valley. Spring came there, not creeping in, not bashful. It started one evening with a warm south wind sweeping in over the mountains, gentle to start with, but increasing in strength during the night. In the morning's bright warm sun, a small creek began to creep out over the mountainside. Soon another appeared, then a third —and soon more, all over the south side.

Then in the afternoon, the mountain on the north side started to pour it on, and creek after creek crept out all around the precipitous mountains, some big, some small, some looking like white strings hanging down from the very top; others, big and powerful, thundering out between lofty peaks, hanging like gigantic icicles upside down. The fog from the waterfalls, drifting with the wind, shone in the sun in all the rainbow's colors. The rumble, roar and crash was so overwhelming that nobody could talk. It was impossible to hear anything else above the noise. It was a revolution—the south wind and sun against the cold, nasty old winter.

This was spring in all its glory, bubbling, boiling all over the valley. The thundering waterfalls changed their tune from time to time. They rumbled and roared. The young people could not stand still. They all were smiling, laughing and dancing. Young and old, they had to be outside. It was like a great tonic, a celebration! It twinkled and quivered all over inside of you. You did not walk, you ran and leaped. You were too excited to eat or sleep. It was spring, that glorious time folks in the valley long for. Now they were sailing on white clouds towards warm, sunny summer days and short nights. That was spring in Norway.

But in North Dakota, what loveliness of another kind! Daybreak on the prairie! The first golden beams from the rising sun painted the skies in a symphony of color and light. The purple and gold filtered through the night's blue haze, often sending a flare of yellow and orange in a long arch. Over the blue velvet sky a lone star sparkled like a diamond in all its splendor.

Then I heard the first strange sound from somewhere—a muffled sound, like that of a musician tuning his instrument—a suppressed tone from a trumpet—a short, clear laughter—and some more tuning. I stood wondering. Is it people or birds or animals? Then came the first booming sound, loud and clear—then another and some more. I am on the run. The sound came from a grass plot in front of an old, run-down house. I followed the road, then across a wet field circling back of the old house, through a hedge and then I crept through the door and over the rotten wooden floor. The window was old with cobwebs hanging down. I brushed aside the webs and cleaned a small spot on the windowpane. Behold, I had a front seat at the prairie chicken's springtime powwow!

The dance was in full swing with tapping feet, booming sounds and cackling laughter — downward-sweeping wings and fan-shaped tail feathers, often standing erect with those glorious blazing colors. The performance lasts for twenty minutes. Then all is quiet. The rooster is gone and so are the hens. Outside the old deserted house there is bright sunshine. Spring is here, not crawling in over the prairie anymore. It marches in with drums and booming sounds. Sometimes a bugle is heard. The wonderful prairie chicken brings spring in all its glory to North Dakota's great state. What a glorious system Nature has! It takes a booming sound that carries for a long distance—the proclamation that it is time to wake up. Outside the old house, the sun rises higher. A mirage appears in the sky —a city with parks and sleepy lagoons, beautiful homes. The houses are so clear in this fata morgana that even the white swans on the lagoon are visible.

It was my great good fortune to have the front seat for the springtime performance every morning—but not alone. It was shared with many youngsters. They will never forget that last curtain-call for the prairie chickens, the lovely creatures' swan song. The roosters had those bulging air sacs on the side of the neck with feathers a bright orange, and when they pressed the air from those sacs there was the booming sound.

Maybe the most fascinating of all was the introduction to dance—so like an airy performer on the stage when the curtain had risen. One bird would run to the center, wings spread out low, nearly touching the ground, with outstretched neck, feet tapping, and bow the head in different directions, like a great performer introducing a wonderful show. With lots of cackling and high-pitched greeting, the dance would start, a show so fascinating that you would forget time and place.

During the summer, I often saw the prairie chickens and their offspring on the road, sleeping or taking a bath in the sun. When we cut the hay in the meadow we often stopped, so that the hen could have a chance to move her chicks out of the way of the mower.

When the summer was gone, harvest time was over and the golden grain was stored in the elevators, the long stubble was left, which supplied good cover and plenty of food for the birds. The prairie chickens gathered in big flocks and moved from one field to another. The young wings had to be hardened for a fast start and a quick flight.

A tractor is tugging three plows. They cut deep furrows in the black, rich soil. A grass snake on his way to hibernation finds the bottom of the furrow easy for traveling, only to be rolled under by the plow turning dirt.

Then! From the west comes an automobile at great speed. The car bounces over the rough dirt road and clouds of dust pour out from the wheels. Ahead of the car is a big flock of prairie chickens in fast flight. They reach a field with long wheat stubble and dive in. The driver of the car stops on a ridge not far from where the chickens land. After a while three more cars sweep in from the west with four men in each open car, the dust clouds drifting over the fields. When they reach the first car, the driver gets out and walks over to the leader. This driver points to exactly the place where the prairie chickens landed. The three cars circle the stubble field and take possession on three sides. At a given signal all three cars, with four men in each, roar in from three sides and meet in the center where the chickens were. The whole flock pours out of the stubble, wings beating the air, up and up in their flight above the automobiles.

The guns start barking, all twelve of them. Salvo after salvo into the winging birds! It sounds like a war! Prairie chickens tumble from the sky. It rains birds. It is a mass destruction. Not one-half of the flock gets away from this hell. The few that were left head east; and so also does the fourth auto. It follows the flock and the driver notices where the birds land. The men from the three autos pick up what birds they can find in a hurry, throw them into their cars and roar after the other car to where the remaining chickens are landing. Here again, the same procedure is repeated for the mass destruction of the prairie chicken, a systematic slaughtering on one section of land after the other.

The American Indians had a dance that was an imitation of the prairie chicken, with swift running and arms feathered like wings, sweeping low, with feet tapping gaily and madly. They danced, and danced rapturously, because for the Indians the prairie chicken was a favorite, the most beloved bird of all. I am sure it was not the Indians who slaughtered the prairie chickens.

It was my sad lot to gather up many of the birds that were left—some dead, some crippled, broken wings, legs missing, some dying in my hands. For me, it was like picking up the crushed pieces of a soft musical instrument that never again would bring Springtime Jubilee to North Dakota's endless prairie.

Years have passed. Many snows have melted on the rich lands there in the north. On some silent nights, I can still hear the springtime booming call from the wide prairie, like an echo from many years ago. No, it is not the prairie chicken's drumming call any more. It is the trumpet's clear tone, sorrowful and lonely, as it sounds the last taps for a wonderful game bird.

A Journey on the Lonesome Trail

From the hard-packed trail, through woods and fields come the thudding noise of wild animals, and also on the move some light-footed creatures in an endless stream. Overhead all kinds of ducks and geese are in flight to somewhere, wings beating the air, and the honks from the geese are so overwhelming that it drowns all other sounds. I wander through the field and forest where the prairie chicken, the grouse and the Hungarian partridge are sitting, bathing in the sun, and the pheasant with his bright colors is picking sand.

In the distance I can see lots of deer, big and small, and also caribou, yes, even a whole herd of moose browsing in the sun. A beautiful lake, so still, shines like a mirror, where ducks by the thousands are swimming, diving or resting on the shore. Swans, looking so proud, so elegant, float like white clouds over the crystal-clear, blue water. I also notice great crowds of people, happy and glad, snapping pictures of all these beautiful animals and birds. In an opening in the woods a doe and two of her offspring are performing for a bunch of people. The fawns are jumping, dancing and galloping. I cannot understand what has happened? Is this America? And where is all the abundance of animals coming from?

Then through my open window comes the shattering noise of a shotgun blast, four or five shots in quick succession. I am awake. It was only a mirage. The dream is over. That was the first day of the duck season. Now the hunters are prowling all along the marshes, lakes and streams, eager for a chance to kill. If there were an abundance of wild game, then some harvest could be tolerated, but now when so few are left of our precious fauna, it is really hard to understand.

In the future, the young people and even the children will have a different slant on hunting. They will not be able to understand the necessity of all the killing and trying to destroy even the last species. They will also be wondering if the lust to kill is an inherent sickness, or is it a fairy-tale spun from father to son, that to be a man, kill you must? Time will tell if we can save some of our precious wild animals and birds; yes, even fish, for that matter. But it will be a race against time.

Are you with us? Then do something before it is too late!

In Appreciation

This book, "Twilight Over the Wilderness," would not be complete without this gallery of excellent paintings and others throughout this book created by Roger Preuss. It is a sad thing that millions of Americans have not had a chance to see, admire and understand our precious fauna, our fellow travelers on this earth, to know and to love them in their own environment.

Of course to study these paintings is not the same thing as to see the wild animals, birds and fish in life, in their own world. But they will be a cherished collection in time to come when so many of our fauna are no more.

And it certainly would be a great help if millions of our citizens were interested enough to join some of the excellent organizations for the preservation of our fauna. But remember that it must be NOW, not some time in the future. Because the time is tragically short.

My appreciation for the great talent of Roger Preuss, his understanding and dedication in portraying our wonderful wildlife. He is not only an excellent artist but he has studied the wild animals, birds and fish for a lifetime, and so these paintings are indeed true and accurately presented. And also I give my most grateful appreciation for cooperation to those perceptive, nobly intelligent art collectors of Roger Preuss paintings featured in this book.

THE HOMEMAKERS — MOURNING DOVES

Collection of Dr. John P. Kelly

Mourning Doves

Not all our wonderful songbirds sing a happy tune. Some seem to have a tear in the throat like, for instance, the heilos in Norway. Its lonely, sad call can be heard in the summertime over marshes in the high mountain plateaus. Also there is the blue seagull's sorrowful cry over the endless Polar Region. In America, if you are lucky enough, you might hear the mourning dove sobbing his sorrowful "Wou-wu." They all belong in the great songbird's chorale in a world where so very few people take the time to listen to the birds' splendid symphony.

THE WHITE-TAILED PTARMIGAN

Collection of Wildlife of America

The White-Tailed Ptarmigan

The handsome bird of this painting is solely an American. He is a bird of our high western mountains. He belongs mostly to the northern states, Washington, Idaho, western Montana and the towering western Colorado mountains. He changes his color with the season and often will look like the background—in winter pure white and then changing through spring and summer to a darkish mottled hue so as to be nearly invisible in his surroundings.

THE WHITE-TAILED DEER

L. C. Smith Collection

The White-Tailed Deer

In the wild animals' world, thousands are born and thousands die every year. Only the strong and healthy will live, and they have what it takes. They are the breeding stock of tomorrow. The deer is no exception. From the time they are born they are harassed by predators and, later in life, hunted by men. They are in the cruel, rugged Northwest with blustery winters, deep snow and strong winds—so hard for the full-grown and almost impossible for the young ones to plow through the deep snow to reach food. The deer is a beautiful animal with lots of class, an elegant appearance and a movement of indescribable grace. Not all men have the heart to kill a beautiful creature like the deer.

LARGEMOUTH BASS — FEEDING TIME
Collection of William B. Randall

The Largemouthed Bass

One of the best places to go to get away from it all is to go fishing on a beautiful sunny summer day. We do this, not to get the limit of fish, but to enjoy the stillness of the lake, the beautiful landscape and to be lulled nearly to sleep by the gentle waves cradling the boat. Forgotten are the big problems, the nerve-tearing pressure and the important decisions. Here on the lake, man is in harmony with nature.

THE MOUNTAIN GOAT

The Thomas D. Murphy Company

The Mountain Goat

The Mountain King would be a more fitting name for this great monarch as he stands on a narrow mountain shelf, thousands of feet up, spying over the rugged landscape, his kingdom. Green fields and deep woods are not his joys in living. He prefers the high mountain life. Free, independent, sure-footed is he! He is the king of the mountains and the absolute ruler of his world!

THE BADGER

The Thomas D. Murphy Company

The Badger

Some people would say that the badger is not a beautiful animal, and they may be right. He is quite flat in appearance and somewhat too broad and low-slung, and besides that, he is bowlegged and pigeon-toed. It does not matter much to him. For him the looks are not too important. He is one of the world's best diggers, and after all, the great Designer was right as always when He created the badger.

THE MOOSE — The Thomas D. Murphy Company

The Moose

No wonder he is called the "King of the Forest." So majestic he looks, so dignified and grand! He is the mogul of the forest and he knows it. But look out when he sometimes comes crashing through the woods, higher than a horse, head outstretched, his heavy antlers ripping big branches right and left, and knocking over small trees like bowling pins. He is tremendous! Even seasoned hunters tremble when he unexpectedly comes thundering through the woods. He is hot-tempered and ugly when wounded or trapped, majestic and noble when he raises his great head with the lofty crown, for his last look over his kingdom.

THE BOBCAT

The Thomas D. Murphy Company

The Bobcat

He is not a house cat and would rarely give up his freedom to become a house pet. He is a predator in the forest, but often he prefers to stay close to people's homes. Powerfully built, with excellent coordination, he is a match for most of the forestland's inhabitants. He is hard to see and track down, mysterious and vanishing almost like a ghost.

THE MOUNTAIN QUAIL Collection of Wildlife of America

The Mountain Quail

He is not named the mountain quail for nothing. He is a bird of the rugged, high terrain from 2500 feet up, and the more removed the better. He is hard to find and not easily reached to hunt. He also is an excellent runner and always sprints uphill. The tall black plumes raise majestically like royal banners over his handsome head.

THE PRAIRIE DOG   The Thomas D. Murphy Company

The Prairie Dog

He is not one of the impressive creatures, but he is an important link in nature's cycle, because when the humans invaded the prairie they nearly destroyed him, and also the rich wildlife on the open plains disappeared. The prairie dog is a very important link for all living things. It seems to me we now have created too many missing links in this country, and we have not changed our ways and methods. We still are destroying our fellow-travelers on this earth at a fast clip with no letup in sight.

THE STRIPED SKUNK

Collection of Wildlife of America

The Striped Skunk

He is a rather attractive, defenseless-looking creature that usually likes man and his vicinity and he makes a cuddly pet. Yes, an excellent pet for children and also for young people. Of course, the dogs and cats of the family will not share the children's love for him because of the odor he sometimes carries along. He always has had a somewhat difficult and cumbersome life.

THE RED FOX

Michaels Collection

The Red Fox

He is a very clever animal and smart because he has been and is now born in a world of enemies. He has been forced to pit his wits against the brutal force of man. He has withstood human treachery and has been chased by packs of hunters on horseback. He has had to look out for traps, snares and poison, and besides all that, the man and his dogs. He is positive in his opinion that he was here before men came. And furthermore, what right have the humans to destroy all wildlife? Just look at the human beings—the terrible mess they have created!